Let Us Now Praise Famous Gardens

1. *Voices of Akenfield* Ronald Blythe
2. *The Wood* John Stewart Collis
3. *From Dover to the Wen* William Cobbett
4. *The Pleasures of English Food* Alan Davidson
5. *Through England on a Side-Saddle* Celia Fiennes
6. *Elegy Written in a Country Churchyard and Other Poems* Various
7. *A Shropshire Lad* A. E. Housman
8. *Cathedrals and Castles* Henry James
9. *Walks in the Wheat-fields* Richard Jefferies
10. *The Beauties of a Cottage Garden* Gertrude Jekyll
11. *Country Churches* Simon Jenkins
12. *A Wiltshire Diary* Francis Kilvert
13. *Some Country Houses and their Owners* James Lees-Milne
14. *The Clouded Mirror* L. T. C. Rolt
15. *Let Us Now Praise Famous Gardens* Vita Sackville-West
16. *One Green Field* Edward Thomas
17. *English Folk Songs* Ralph Vaughan Williams and A. L. Lloyd
18. *Country Lore and Legends* Jennifer Westwood and Jacqueline Simpson
19. *Birds of Selborne* Gilbert White
20. *Life at Grasmere* Dorothy and William Wordsworth

LET US NOW PRAISE FAMOUS GARDENS

Vita
Sackville-West

English Journeys

PENGUIN BOOKS

Published by the Penguin Group
Penguin Books Ltd, 80 Strand, London WC2R ORL, England
Penguin Group (USA) Inc., 375 Hudson Street, New York, New York 10014, USA
Penguin Group (Canada), 90 Eglinton Avenue East, Suite 700, Toronto, Ontario, Canada M4P 2Y3
(a division of Pearson Penguin Canada Inc.)
Penguin Ireland, 25 St Stephen's Green, Dublin 2, Ireland
(a division of Penguin Books Ltd)
Penguin Group (Australia), 250 Camberwell Road, Camberwell, Victoria 3124, Australia
(a division of Pearson Australia Group Pty Ltd)
Penguin Books India Pvt Ltd, 11 Community Centre, Panchsheel Park, New Delhi – 110 017, India
Penguin Group (NZ), 67 Apollo Drive, Rosedale, North Shore 0632, New Zealand
(a division of Pearson New Zealand Ltd)
Penguin Books (South Africa) (Pty) Ltd, 24 Sturdee Avenue, Rosebank, Johannesburg 2196, South Africa

Penguin Books Ltd, Registered Offices: 80 Strand, London WC2R ORL, England

www.penguin.com

This selection taken from *In Your Garden*, first published by Michael Joseph 1951
Published in Penguin Books 2009

3

Copyright © Vita Sackville-West, 1951
All rights reserved

Set by Rowland Phototypesetting Ltd, Bury St Edmunds, Suffolk
Printed in England by Clays Ltd, St Ives plc

ISBN: 978-0-141-19089-1

www.greenpenguin.co.uk

January

January 1, 1950

Some generous friend may have given you a plant-token for Christmas, and you may be wondering, as I am now wondering, how best to expend it. A plant-token is a real gift from heaven; it represents an extravagance one might hesitate to commit for oneself; a luxury, an extra, a treat. One has no alternative, for, unlike a cheque, one cannot virtuously put it to the reduction of one's overdraft. There is nothing to be done with it except to buy a plant.

Could one do better than choose the autumn-flowering cherry, *Prunus subhirtella autumnalis*? In England it might more properly be called winter-flowering, for it does not open until November, but in its native Japan it begins a month earlier; hence its autumnal name. Here, if you pick it in the bud and put it in a warm room or a greenhouse, you can have the white sprays in flower six weeks before Christmas, and it will go on intermittently, provided you do not allow the buds to be caught by too severe a frost, until March.

It is perhaps too ordinary to appeal to the real connoisseur – a form of snobbishness I always find hard to understand in gardeners – but its wands of white are of so delicate and graceful a growth, whether on the tree or in a vase, that it surely should not be condemned on that account. It is of the easiest cultivation, content with any reasonable soil, and it may be grown either as a standard or a bush; I think the bush is preferable, because then you get the flowers at eye-level instead of several feet above your head – though it can also look very frail and youthful, high up against the pale blue of a winter sky.

How precious are the flowers of mid-winter! Not the hot house things, nor even the forced trusses of lilac, most of which, I understand, come from Holland, but the genuine toughs that for some strange reason elect to display themselves out-of-doors at this time of year. The Winter-sweet opens its yellow star-fish against a wall, and the twisted ribbons of the Witch-hazel are disentangling themselves on their leafless branches. Both of these sweet-scented winter flowerers should qualify for a choice with the plant-token.

Garrya elliptica is not so often seen, though it has been known in this country since 1818; its nickname, the Tassel Bush, describes it best, for it hangs itself from December onwards with soft grey-green catkins eight or ten inches in length, like bunches of enormous caterpillars among the very dark leaves. Some people think it dismal, but a large bush is an imposing sight if you have the patience to wait for it. It does require patience, for it dislikes being moved and, therefore, must be planted small; also you must insist upon getting a male plant, or there will not be any catkins. The female plant will give you only bunches of black fruits. As it will thrive against a north wall, however, where few other things will thrive, it may well be left there to take its time without occupying the space wanted for something else.

January 15, 1950

Someone has been pleading with me to put in a good word for sweet-briar. I do so most willingly, for a hedge of sweet-briar is one of the most desirable things in any garden.

It is thorny enough to keep out intruders, should it be needed as a boundary protection; in early summer it is as pretty as the dog-rose, with its pale pink single flowers; in autumn it turns itself into a sheer wall of scarlet hips; and on moist muggy evenings after rain the scent is really and truly strong in the ambient air. You do not need to crush a leaf between your fingers to provoke the scent: it swells out towards you of its own accord, as you walk past, like a great sail filling suddenly with a breeze off those Spice Islands which Columbus hoped to find.

These are many virtues to claim, but even so we may add to them. It is the Eglantine of the poets, if you like that touch of romance. True, Milton seems to have confused it with something else, probably the honey-suckle:

> . . . through the sweet-briar or the Vine,
> Or the twisted Eglantine . . .

but what does that matter? it is pedantic to be so precise, and we should do better to take a hint from Milton and plant a *mixed* hedge of honeysuckle and sweet-briar, with perhaps an ornamental vine twining amongst them – the purple-leafed vine, *Vitis vinifera purpurea*, would look sumptuous among the red hips in October.

I have never seen a hedge of this composition; but why not? Ideas come to one; and it remains only to put them into practice. The nearest that I have got is to grow the common *Clematis Jackmanii* into my sweet-briar, planting the clematis on the north side of the hedge, where the roots are cool and shaded and the great purple flowers come wriggling through southwards into the sun. It looks fine, and the briar gives the clematis just the twiggy kind of support it needs.

Sweet-briar is a strong grower, but is often blamed for going thin and scraggy towards the roots. I find that you can correct this weakness by planting your hedge in the first instance against a system of post-and-wire, and subsequently tying-in the long shoots to the posts and wire instead of pruning them. Tie the shoots horizontally, or bend them downwards if need be, thus obtaining a thick, dense growth, which well compensates you for the initial trouble of setting up the posts and the wire. They will last for years, and so will the briar.

The common sweet-briar will cost you 2s. 6d. to 3s. a plant, and the single plant will spread, horizontally, twenty feet or more. The Penzance hybrid briars are more expensive, 4s. 6d. to 5s. each. *Amy Robsart*, with deep rose flowers, and *Lady Penzance*, with coppery-yellow flowers, are particularly to be recommended.

January 22, 1950

It is amusing to make one-colour gardens. They need not necessarily be large, and they need not necessarily be enclosed, though the enclosure of a dark hedge is, of course, ideal. Failing this, any secluded corner will do, or even a strip of border running under a wall, perhaps the wall of the house. The site chosen must depend upon the general lay-out, the size of the garden, and the opportunities offered. And if you think that one colour would be monotonous, you can have a two- or even a three-colour, provided the colours are happily married, which is sometimes easier of achievement in the vege-table than in the human world. You can have, for instance, the blues and the purples, or the yellows and the bronzes, with their attendant mauves and orange, respectively. Personal taste alone will dictate what you choose.

For my own part, I am trying to make a grey, green, and white garden. This is an experiment which I ardently hope may be successful, though I doubt it. One's best ideas seldom play up in practice to one's expectations, especially in gardening, where everything looks so well on paper and in the catalogues, but fails so lamentably in fulfilment after you have tucked your plants into the soil. Still, one hopes.

My grey, green, and white garden will have the advan-tage of a high yew hedge behind it, a wall along one side, a strip of box edging along another side, and a path of old brick along the fourth side. It is, in fact, nothing

more than a fairly large bed, which has now been divided
into halves by a short path of grey flagstones terminating
in a rough wooden seat. When you sit on this seat, you
will be turning your backs to the yew hedge, and from
there I hope you will survey a low sea of grey clumps of
foliage, pierced here and there with tall white flowers. I
visualize the white trumpets of dozens of Regale lilies,
grown three years ago from seed, coming up through
the grey of southernwood and artemisia and cotton-
lavender, with grey-and-white edging plants such as
Dianthus Mrs Sinkins and the silvery mats of *Stachys
Lanata*, more familiar and so much nicer under its English
names of Rabbits' Ears or Saviour's Flannel. There will
be white pansies, and white peonies, and white irises
with their grey leaves . . . at least, I hope there will be
all these things. I don't want to boast in advance about
my grey, green, and white garden. It may be a terrible
failure. I wanted only to suggest that such experiments
are worth trying, and that you can adapt them to your
own taste and your own opportunities.

All the same, I cannot help hoping that the great
ghostly barn-owl will sweep silently across a pale garden,
next summer, in the twilight – the pale garden that I am
now planting, under the first flakes of snow.

January 14, 1951

January seems the wrong time of year to think of planting
bulbs, but there are some which should be planted in
March or April, so this is the moment to order them. I

would recommend the Kaffir Lily, officially called *Schizostylis coccinea*, with its pretty pink variety called *Mrs Hegarty*. It resembles a miniature gladiolus, and it has the advantage, from our point of view, of flowering in October and November, when it is difficult to find anything out of doors for indoor picking.

The Kaffir Lily will cost you anything from seven shillings to eight or nine shillings a dozen. One dozen will give you a good return, if you plant them in the right sort of place and look after them properly. Planting them in the right sort of place means giving them a light, well-drained soil in full sun. Looking after them properly means that you must give them plenty of water during their growing period, when their leaves are throwing up, rather as you would treat an amaryllis, the Belladonna lily. You should realize that they are not entirely hardy, especially in our colder counties; but they are reasonably hardy in most parts of England; a thin quilt of bracken or dry leaves next winter will keep them safe for years. It is remarkable what a little covering of bracken will do for bulbs. Speaking for myself, I cannot imagine anything less adequate than a draughty scatter of bracken on a frosty night, give me a thick eiderdown and blankets every time, and a hot-water bottle, too, but bulbs which are buried deep down in the earth will keep themselves warm and safe with the thinnest cover from frost above them.

Another bulb, or corm, you should order now and plant in March is *Tigridia*, the Mexican Tiger-flower. This is a wildly beautiful exotic-looking thing. It throws only one flower at a time, and that flower lasts only one day, but it is of such superlative beauty and is succeeded by so many other blooms, day after day, that it is well worth the 3s. 9d. you will have to pay for a dozen of mixed varieties. A sunny place is essential, and, like dahlias, they should be lifted and stored through the winter.

January 21, 1951

This is the time to think of ordering bulbs of the autumn-flowering crocus. If the nurseryman knows his job, they will not be sent to you until midsummer or even August, but it is advisable to order now in case the supply runs out, or, to put it in more familiar language, get in at the top of the queue.

We are so well accustomed to associating crocuses with Spring that it may come as a surprise to some people to learn that some sorts of crocus will flower with as vernal an appearance from September onwards into November. *Crocus speciosus* is one that should be ordered now; it is cheap to buy, 2s. 6d. a dozen, 17s. 6d. a hundred; I bought a dozen last year and how lovely they were, chalices the colour of Parma violets rejoicing my autumnal heart, coming out in September so unexpectedly to turn autumn into spring. *C. speciosus Cassiopea* comes out later, October–November; *C. speciosus globosus* in November, the latest of all. These are both a little more expensive than the type, at 3s. 6d. a dozen; but do plant even a little patch of six or twelve, in a special corner.

Then there is *Crocus sativus*, the Saffron crocus, a pinkish-lilac colour. How difficult these colour descriptions are! This flowers in October, and costs from 2s. 6d. to 3s. a dozen. If you want something more unusual, there is *C. asturicus atropurpureus*, dark violet, which in a mild winter might go on flowering into December, 4s. a dozen. I am sorry these small things should have to suffer such gigantic names; but when you work it out, you find that *Crocus asturicus atropurpureus* merely means the very dark purple crocus, native to the Asturias province of northern Spain.

I have by no means exhausted the list, and have not even touched on the *Colchicum*, which many people are apt to confuse with the autumn-flowering crocus. The only point in common, for those who do not want to be bothered with botanical differences, is that they should both be ordered now for August delivery. Owing to what we have been taught to call shortages of newsprint, I shall have to leave the *Colchicum* till next Sunday, when I can devote my four hundred words to this most lovely and surprising race. Messrs. Wallace, Messrs. Barr, and Mr Ralph Cusack all have good lists of the crocus and the *Colchicum*.

I have no means of thanking the anonymous sender of a registered packet addressed to me; but if he should happen to be a reader of these articles, will he please accept my unspeakable thanks? He (or she?) will understand.

January 28, 1951

The colchicums, as I said, should be ordered now for summer delivery. They are more expensive than the crocuses, ranging from 6s. 6d. to 10s. 6d. a dozen, but being larger they make more effect. A drift of them, especially in grass, is a brilliant sight in September and October; they should not be planted on a lawn, as the big leaves which appear in spring or early summer are unsightly; and do not plant them where sheep or cattle graze, as they are poisonous to animals. The ideal place is an orchard, where their pink or lilac cups will coincide with the apples hanging overhead, but if the grass is rough remember to cut it just before the flowers break through or they will be lost to sight. The end of August is a safe time for this operation.

They do not object to a little light shade, such as would be thrown by the fruit trees, but they are equally happy in full sun. It may surprise you that a bulb planted in July or August should leap into flower so soon after-wards, and it may surprise you even more to find that when the bulbs arrive in their paper bag they should already be showing a bleached-looking growth, rather like celery. Do not worry. Cut a hole in the turf, drop the bulbs in, two to three inches deep, stamp the turf down again, and leave them to do what nature intended.

Speciosum and *autumnale* are both good varieties, rosy in colour; there are white forms of these also. *Bornmulleri* and *byzantinus* are magnificent; and one of the finest is the hybrid *Lilac Wonder*, rather more expensive at

10s. 6d. a dozen. Other very fine hybrids are *Rosy Dawn*, bright pink; and *The Giant*, a softer pink; and you can also obtain a mixture of the new hybrids at 10s. 6d. a dozen. I do not care so much for the double-flowered kind, *autumnale roseum plenum*, since I think the beauty of a colchicum or of a crocus, apart from the colour, lies in the pure lines of the goblet-like shape; this, like many other things, is a matter of taste.

A word of practical advice: put a ring of slug bait round each clump as soon as the pale noses appear, and be quick about it, because the pale nose of to-day is the full flower of to-morrow. Otherwise you will wonder how anyone could ever recommend a thing of such rags and tatters.

February

February 1948

It is agreeable sometimes to turn for a change from dutifully practical aspects of gardening to the consideration of something strange, whether we can hope to grow it for ourselves or not. A wet January evening seemed just the time for such an indulgence of dreams, and in an instant I found my room (which hitherto had boasted only a few modest bulbs in bowls) filling up with flowers of the queerest colours, shapes, and habits. The first batch to appear, thus miraculously conjured out of the air, were all of that peculiar blue-green which one observes in verdigris on an old copper, in a peacock's feather, on the back of a beetle, or in the sea where the shallows meet the deep.

First came a slender South African, *Ixia viridiflora*, with green flowers shot with cobalt blue and a purple splotch: this I had once grown in a very gritty pan in a cold green house, and was pleased to see again. Then came the tiny sea-green Persian iris, only three inches high, which I had seen piercing its native desert but had never persuaded into producing a single flower here. Then came *Delphinium macrocentrum*, an East African, which I had never seen at all, but which is said to rival the Chilean *Puya alpestris* in colouring.

Puya alpestris I knew. A ferocious-looking plant, and reluctant. Seven years had I cherished that thing in a pot, before it finally decided to flower. Then it threw up a spike and astonished everybody with its wicked-looking peacock trumpets and orange anthers, and side-shoots on which, apparently, humming-birds were supposed to perch and pollinate the flower.

And now here it was again, in my room, this time accompanied by the humming-birds which had been lamentably absent when I had flowered it after seven years. There were quite a lot of birds in my room by now, as well as flowers. For *Strelitzia reginae* had also arrived, escorted by the little African sun-birds which perch and powder their breast-feathers with its pollen. It is rare for plants to choose birds as pollinators instead of insects; and here were two of them. *Strelitzia reginae* itself looked like a bird, a wild, crested, pointed bird, floating on an orange boat under spiky sails of blue and orange. Although it had been called regina after Queen Charlotte the consort of George III, I preferred it under its other name, the Bird of Paradise Flower.

Then, as a change to homeliness, came clumps of the old primroses I had tried so hard to grow in careful mixtures of leaf-mould and loam, but here they were, flourishing happily between the cracks of the floor-boards. Jack-in-the-Green, Prince Silverwings, Galli-gaskins, Tortoiseshell, Cloth of Gold; and as I saw them there in a wealth I had never been able to achieve, I remembered that the whole primula family was gre-garious in its tastes and hated the loneliness of being one solitary, expensive little plant. They like huddling together, unlike the Lichens, which demand so little company that they will grow (in South America at any rate) strung out along the high isolation of telegraph wires.

There seemed indeed no end to the peculiarities of plants, whether they provided special perches for the convenience of their visitors, or turned carnivorous like the Pitcher-plants. Why was it that the Vine grew from left to right in the Northern hemisphere, but refused to grow otherwise than from right to left in the Southern? Why was the poppy called *Macounii* found only on one tiny Arctic island in the Behring Sea and nowhere else in the world? How had it come there in the first place? In a room now overcrowded with blooms of the imagination such speculations flowed easily, to the exclusion of similar speculations on the equally curious behaviour of men.

The walls of the room melted away, giving place to a garden such as the Emperors of China once enjoyed, vast in extent, varied in landscape, a garden in which everything throve and the treasures of the earth were collected in beauty and brotherhood. But a log fell in the fire: a voice said: 'This is the BBC Home Service; here is the news,' and I awoke.

February 26, 1950

A dear near neighbour brought me a tussie-mussie this week. The dictionary defines tuzzy-muzzy, or tussie-mussie, as *a bunch or posy of flowers, a nosegay*, and then disobligingly adds that the word is obsolete. I refuse to regard it as obsolete. It is a charming word; I have always used it and shall continue to use it, whatever the great *Oxford Dictionary* may say; and shall now take my neighbour's tussie-mussie as a theme to show what ingenuity, taste, and knowledge can produce from a small garden even in February.

My neighbour has many difficulties to contend with. She is not young, she is into her seventh decade. She has no help in her house. Her garden is wind-swept, and the soil is a stiff Weald of Kent clay. (Only those who have tried to garden on Wealden clay can appreciate what that means.) A jobbing gardener from time to time is all that she commands. She does most of the work herself. Yet she manages to produce a bunch such as I will now describe to you.

It is composed of at least five different flowers, all perfectly chosen. She goes always for the best, which I am sure is the secret of good gardening: choose always the best of any variety you want to grow. Thus, in the bunch she brought me, the violets were *pink* violets, the sort called *Coeur d'Alsace*, and the one *Iris Reticulata* she put in was the sort called *Hercules*, which is redder than the familiar purple and gold. The grape-hyacinths were the small sky-blue *azureus*, which flowers earlier and is prettier than the dark blue later sort. The crocus in her bunch was not the common yellow, but had brown markings on its outside; I think it may be *C. susianus* or it may be Moonlight, but I forgot to ask her. The anemone that she put in must be a freakishly early bloom of *Anemone St Bavo*, amethyst petals with an electric-blue centre. How wise she is to grow *Anemone St Bavo* instead of the coarser *Anemone St Brigid*.

The moral of this article, if any newspaper article may have a moral, is that it just shows what you can do if you put your mind to it. I have received many letters saying: 'Do tell us what we can do in a small garden.' My neighbour's tussie-mussie is the answer. She grows those exquisite things in a small, quarter-of-an-acre grassy space under apple trees, and somehow produces a jewelled effect rather like the foreground of Botticelli's *Primavera*. They are all low and brilliant and tiny; and no more difficult to grow than their more ordinary relations.

Some day I must write an article describing the way my neighbour has designed her garden; and also, perhaps, what she manages to do with her small, unheated greenhouse. You would be surprised.

February 4, 1951

I notice that people become enraged over the names of plants, and I don't wonder. I wish only that they would not blame it on me. 'Why,' they write indignantly, 'why can't you give us a good honest English name instead of all this Latin?' Well, whenever there is an English name, I do give it; I prefer it myself; I would much rather call a thing Bouncing Bet than *Saponaria officinalis*; but when there is no name in the vernacular, our common speech, what am I to do?

Instead of getting cross about it, we should do better to take an intelligent interest in discovering what lies behind these apparently appalling names. There is always a reason, and the best reason is that by using an international idiom, such as Latin, botanists and gardeners can understand one another all the world over. If I see that a plant is described as *azureus* I know instantly that it is blue, and so does my opposite number in Brazil, France, or Pakistan. If it is described as *azureus vernus*, I know that it is not only blue, but that it flowers in the spring. Then if you want to indicate what explorer first found it, you tack on, say, *Farreri*, or *Fortunei*, which we can all manage, or *Mlokosewitchii*, which perhaps we can't.

There appear to be two principal grievances. I hope I have disposed of the first one, but I do suggest that some society such as the Royal Horticultural Society might supply an inexpensive alphabetical glossary for easy reference. If such a thing exists, I do not know of it. It would be a great convenience; we should all rush to look up *strobiliformis* or *quintuplinervius*, only to discover that it meant *shaped like a fir-cone*, and *five-veined* in the description of a leaf.

The second grievance concerns changes of botanical name. I admit that it is very puzzling to be brought up in our childhood to call lilac *lilac*, and syringa *syringa*, and now suddenly to be told in our middle-age that we must call lilac *syringa* and syringa *philadelphus*; but here again there is a good respect-worthy reason, in the attempt either to get back to the first names given by earlier botanists, or to define a new botanical classification, in the interest of accuracy and in the avoidance of confusion.

All the same, sentimentally, Bet may bounce as happily as she likes over my garden, and all her friends, too.

March

March 9, 1947

A pot of cyclamen is a favourite Christmas present, and very nice, too, but by this time (March) some recipients may be wondering what to do with it. Don't throw it away. It will repeat its beauty for you year after year if you treat it right. Treating it right means (1) keeping it moist so long as it continues to flower and to carry leaves; (2) letting it dry off by degrees after the last buds have opened and faded away; (3) keeping it, still in its pot, *unwatered*, in a frost-proof place during the remaining cold weeks, and then standing it out of doors, still unwatered, still in its pot, throughout the spring and early summer in a shady place; (4) starting it into life again in July or August. Starting it into life again merely means giving it water again – very simple. It will then begin, quite quickly, to show new buds all over the corm; but to get the best out of it you ought then to re-pot it. It likes a rather loose soil, made up of fibrous loam, some gritty sand, and a handful of bonemeal, all mixed well together. *Do not bury the corm*; it should sit on top, three-quarters visible. Do not water too much at first, water more generously when autumn comes and you bring your pots into the shelter of a warm greenhouse if you have one; or on to a warm window-sill if you have not.

Do not ever, at any time, give too much water. If you do, your plant will very quickly notify you by turning its leaves yellow and by developing a soft rot in the stems of the flowers. There seem to be two schools of thought about the best way to water. Some growers say it is better to avoid overhead watering which may cause the corm to rot, and that it is better to stand the pot in a saucer or bowl with an inch or so of water, thus absorbing the moisture through the porous pot up into the roots, remembering to empty the water away when you think the plant has had enough. Other growers condemn the saucer idea.

A cottage friend of mine who grows some superb cyclamen on her kitchen window-sill tells me that her grandmother advised her to water them with weak tea. This may sound like an old wife's tale, but the tales of some old wives sometimes turn out to be right.

There are two kinds of cyclamen: the Persian, which is the one your friends give you, and which is not hardy, and the small, out-door one, a tiny edition of the big Persian, as hardy as a snowdrop. These little cyclamen are among the longest-lived of garden plants. A cyclamen corm will keep itself going for more years than its owner is likely to live. They have other advantages: (1) they will grow under trees, for they tolerate, and indeed enjoy, shade; (2) they do not object to a limy soil; (3) they will seed themselves and (4) they will take you round the calendar by a judicious planting of different sorts. *C. neapolitanum*, for instance, will precede its ivy-like leaves by its little pink flower in late autumn, white flowers if you get the variety *album*; *C. coum*, pink, white, or lilac, will flower from December to March; *C. ibericum* from February to the end of March; *C. balearicum* will then carry on, followed by *C. repandum*, which takes you into the summer; and, finally, *C. europæum* for the late summer and early autumn. Some botanists believe this to be a native; it was certainly recorded here in the reign of Queen Elizabeth, when, if beaten into little flat cakes, it was considered 'a good amorous medicine to make one in love'.

Anyone who grows the little cyclamen will have observed that they employ an unusual method of twiddling a kind of corkscrew, or coil, to project the seeds from the capsule when ready. One would imagine that the coil would go off with a ping, rather like the mainspring of a clock when one overwinds it, thus flinging the seeds far and wide, and this indeed was the theory put forward by many botanists. It would appear, however, that nothing of the kind happens, and that the seeds are gently deposited on the parent corm. Why, then, this elaborate apparatus of the coil, if it serves only to drop the seed on to a hard corm and not on to the soft receptive soil? It has been suggested, notably by Mr A. T. Johnson, that this concentration of the seeds may be Nature's idea of providing a convenient little heap for some distributing agent to carry away, and he points out that ants may be seen, in later summer, hurrying off with the seeds until not one is left. I confess that I have never sat up with a cyclamen long enough to watch this curious phenomenon of the exploding capsule; and I still wonder how and why seedlings so obligingly appear in odd corners of the garden – never, I must add, very far away from the parent patch.

You may find some of them a little difficult to obtain now, but *C. europæum*, *coum*, and *neapolitanum* are still listed by nurserymen, and are the three varieties I would recommend for a start. So accommodating are they that you can plant them at almost any time, though ideally they should be planted when dormant, i.e. in June or July. Messrs. Barr & Sons, King Street, Covent Garden, London, WC2, have a good list.

March 6, 1950

Successful gardening is not necessarily a question of wealth. It is a question of love, taste, and knowledge. The neighbour about whom I was writing on page 16 possesses all these virtues, added to fingers so green that the water must surely turn emerald in the basin every time she washes her hands. There are two things I should like to describe to you in connection with my neighbour: one is the way she has designed her garden, and the other is the way she makes use of her small greenhouse.

Which shall I take first? The greenhouse, perhaps, since this is the time of the year when one can make the best use of a greenhouse for growing seeds and for producing a display of flowers. My neighbour does both, and does it in the most unconventional fashion. It would make any professional gardener laugh, and would send him away scratching his head with a lot to think over. She does the oddest things. She digs up clumps of violets from her outdoor garden and has them blooming exuberantly in pots, the small pink violet and the little almost-blue one; and as she takes the trouble to whitewash her pots, instead of leaving them to their normal hideous terra-cotta colour, you may imagine how the flowers gain in beauty as they pour over those blanched containers, white and clean as blancoed tennis-shoes. She digs up clumps of snowdrops and crocuses, and packs them into an ordinary pudding basin. One end of the house is all flowers and colour; the side-stagings are devoted to seed boxes.

She has not many real wooden seed boxes. There are cardboard dress-boxes tied round with string to prevent them from disintegrating, and old Golden Syrup tins, and even some of those tall tins that once contained Slug-death, and some of those little square chip-baskets called punnets. I verily believe that she would use an old shoe if it came handy. In this curious assortment of receptacles an equally curious assortment of seedlings are coming up, green as a lawn, prolific as mustard-and-cress on a child's bit of flannel. There are cabbages and lettuces in some of them; rare lilies in others; and I noted a terrified little crop of auriculas scurrying up, as though afraid that they might be late for a pricking-out into the warm earth of May.

It all goes to show what you can do if you try, in gardening. There are such possibilities, not necessarily expensive.

I was half mistaken, by the way, in describing this greenhouse as unheated. It *is* unheated as a rule, but on a chilly evening when a threat of frost is in the air an electric tube underneath the staging can be turned on by means of a switch located in the kitchen. What could be simpler? No need to bother with a stoke-hole or paraffin radiators; no need to go out into the cold night. It is rather an extravagant method, but that it is clean and labour-saving cannot be denied.

March 12, 1950

This is going to be about designing a small garden. By a small garden I mean anything from half an acre to two acres. It is a big subject to tackle in so short an article. I can hope only to give a few general ideas.

The small garden may be a bungalow garden, or a council-house garden, or the garden round an old cottage, or the garden round a new house on a main bus route. Whichever it is, the true gardener will wish to make the most of the patch of the planet Earth at his personal and particular command. In most cases his design will be dictated by the shape of his patch, and by the position of his dwelling-house in it: thus, he may feel compelled to have a straight path running from the front gate to the front door, and to arrange his flower-beds, his borders, and his bit of lawn accordingly, in which case his garden will look exactly like his next-door-neighbour's garden. What I would like to suggest is that a little ingenuity can vary the pattern.

I have three gardens in mind. One of them has been constructed in front of a small house facing the road. It has been turned into a landscape garden on a miniature scale. The path does not run straight from the front gate to the front door but wanders round sideways, and the middle part of the front garden is occupied by a deep pool surrounded by weeping willows and *Iris Sibirica*, reflecting their pale mauve and their deep purple into the water. Some Irish yews have also been planted; and they now reflect their images into the pool, duplicating themselves in the watery mirror and making this tiny garden look twice the size it is.

My next garden also faces a road, a main road. It would have been easy, and obvious, to turn this into a conventional sort of garden. But the owners have designed it cleverly: they have put it sideways to the house, so that the flower beds, which ought, in the conventional way, to be geometrically set along the house, are put in a surprising way alongside.

My third garden is the sort of garden I like best. It is a cottage-garden of the best sort, kept by a true gardener. This is a garden that slopes rather vaguely downhill towards Romney Marsh, with views of the Marsh beyond it. It is packed with flowers at all times of the year, so exquisitely arranged that they gain their full value wherever they are. I remember specially a planting of the blue primrose mixed with the blue scilla round the base of a grey stone well-head, a perfectly-chosen combination.

March 26, 1950

We now approach the time of year when the thoughts of Man turn towards the pruning of his roses. Knives and secateurs are now at their sharpest. Brandishing these objects of destruction, battalions of professional and amateur gardeners advance, prepared to do their worst, as they have immemorially been taught. The word of command has gone out: 'Cut almost to the ground; cut down to the second or third bud; cut till nothing is left except a couple of inches sticking up. Be pitiless, be ruthless; prune for fine blooms, exhibition blooms, even if you don't intend to exhibit. Never mind about the appearance of your garden, or the natural alacrity of your roses. Snub them as hard as you can, even as Victorian parents snubbed their children.'

It rejoices me to see that different ideas are creeping in. The rose, even the hybrid Teas and the hybrid Perpetuals; is no longer to be regarded as a stunted dwarf, but as a wildly blossoming shrub. Let her grow up, even to three or four feet in height, and throw her head about as I believe that she was meant to. This truth first dawned upon me during the war, when as a Land Army representative I had occasion to visit many small gardens in pursuit of owners who had been called away. Their gardens were turning into a sad disorder of weeds, but the roses reared themselves up, superb and proud, just because they had not been interfered with for two, three, four, five years. Then in the well-kept garden of a friend I saw similar rose bushes which, she assured me, had scarcely been touched since she planted them thirty years ago. She had merely snipped the tips; had taken out the dead wood and the weak growth; and for the rest had left them to their will. The result was lavish and surprising.

My liking for gardens to be lavish is an inherent part of my garden philosophy. I like generosity wherever I find it, whether in gardens or elsewhere. I hate to see things scrimp and scrubby. Even the smallest garden can be prodigal within its own limitations, and I would now suggest that you should try the experiment of NOT slaughtering your roses down to almost ground level, at least for this year; and see what happens.

I know that I have touched only the outskirts of this controversial subject. There is so much to be said, and so many different types of rose to deal with, that it all becomes confused and confusing. Everyone agrees that the hybrid Musk and the species roses are better without the knife, but no doubt the new unorthodoxy about the hybrid Teas will evoke screams of protest. I am prepared to admit that it might not suit them all. The only thing is to be bold; try the experiment; and find out.

April

April 6, 1947

I must start with a warning not to despair about plants apparently killed by the frosts, ice-rain, east winds, and other afflictions they have had to suffer. (Written in April 1947.) They may look dead now, but their powers of revival are astonishing. You may have to cut some shrubs down to ground level, but my recommendation would be not to dig anything up rashly until you are quite, quite certain that it has no intention of putting out green shoots again. This certitude may not come until the summer is well advanced. I remember the agreeable surprises we got after the cruel winter of 1940.

All garden work has been so much delayed that many people will have to rely on generous sowings of annuals this year for extra colour. If you have not time to spare for the ideal method of growing them in boxes and then planting them out, you still have a large choice of those which may be sown straight into the ground. A finely broken soil; sow thinly, not too deep; thin out remorselessly, for most annuals will fill a space from a foot to two feet wide if given the chance, looking sturdy and bushy instead of drawn and spindly; and remember that it is far more effective to sow large patches of a few varieties than small patches of many. What you sow must depend upon your personal taste and the colouring you want. As a change from the usual jumble, pretty and gay though that may be, you might find it more original to concentrate on one colour. A combination of *Phacelia*, *Nigella* (love-in-the-mist), *Nemophila*, *Asperula azurea*, would give a brilliant blue effect, especially if massed in front of delphiniums. Coreopsis, Eschscholtzia, Calendula Orange King and Lemon Queen, Nemesia yellow and orange (not quite hardy) would lie like a pool of sunlight. Mauve and purple stocks, Alyssum Lilac Queen, mauve Candytuft, mauve Godetia, Clarkia Purple Prince, Petunias (not quite hardy), make a sumptuous association. These are only a few suggestions, just enough, I hope, to indicate what scope there is for ingenuity.

April 9, 1950

For once, instead of giving advice, may I ask for it? How does one protect the choicer sorts of primroses from the attack of sparrows? Has any reader of these articles a sovereign remedy against this naughty, wanton, wild destruction? Short of putting automatic cartridges amongst my primroses, I have done everything I can think of. I have made a sort of cat's cradle of strong black thread, pegged down in the hope that the birds would catch their nasty little claws in it as they alighted and thus be frightened and discouraged. It doesn't work. The sparrows don't seem to mind. I can suppose only that they crawl underneath the threads and nip the flowers off, scattering the buds and the heads all over the ground at dawn before I have got up in the morning.

This is a real SOS. I have quite a collection of un-common primroses, Jack-in-the-Green, Madame Pompa-dour, Cloth-of-Gold, and so on, but what is the good of that if the sparrows take them all? I would try not to grudge them their fun if it was of any benefit to them, but it isn't. They are mischievous hooligans who destroy for the sake of destruction.

Some of these old primroses are very charming and there are signs that, like several other old-fashionable flowers, they are coming back into favour. Unfortunately they are neither easy to obtain nor to grow. Sometimes one sees a happy clump of the double white or the double purple in a cottage garden, but then it is a truism that things will flourish without any attention at all in a cottage garden, when all the skill and science of the professional well-instructed gardener leads only to the petering-out of the last miserable sickly survivor. Still, the doubles do not appear to be so choosy, and a half-shady corner with plenty of leaf-mould should suit them. They associate very gladly with their relations the Auriculas, or with the Hepaticas (a kind of anemone), and they are all, I think, plants for an intimate recess where their low beauty may be studied apart from the flauntings of their spring contemporaries such as the daffodils. They need to be observed in the small secret of their chosen shade.

This is all very well, but what am I to do about the sparrows?

*

The Pasque-flower, *Anemone pulsatilla*, is blooming just now, for Easter as its name indicates. This is a native of our Downs, getting rare in its wild state, but still cultivated in gardens. It is a soft and lovely thing, pale lilac in colour with a silvery floss-silk surround: and it can now be obtained also in a rosy-pink colouring, which mixes and merges most exquisitely with the original mauve of the native. Maurice Prichard & Sons, Riverslea Nurseries, Christchurch, Hampshire, specialize in these. There is also a white form. It is easy to grow anywhere, though as a native of the chalk hills it appreciates a bed of limy rubble in the sun.

The sparrows so far, touch wood, have left it alone.

April 16, 1950

When I was small I had a book called *Flowers that do not disappoint*. They nearly all did, but that was probably my fault so far as the annuals were concerned. Hardy annuals should not disappoint, and there is still time to sow them in April, so useful for filling bare patches or for making a display in the window-boxes of town houses.

The charm of annuals is their light gaiety, as though they must make the most of their brief lives to be frivolous and pleasure-giving. They have no time to be austere or glum. They must always be youthful, because they have no time to grow old. And so their colours are bright, and their foliage airy, and their only morality is to be as cheerful as possible, and to leave as much seed as they can behind them for their progeny to continue in the same tradition. This, of course, is the one thing you must not let them do: all seeding heads must ruthlessly be snipped off if you want to prolong the exuberance of flowers.

So much advice has been given about sowing annuals that it is perhaps unnecessary to repeat it in too much detail. The ground should be well dug, but, generally speaking, not over enriched, unless it is very poor. It should be broken down into a fine surface tilth. The piece of advice that people never take is: sow thinly and thin out remorselessly; but if ever you have noticed a solitary plant growing with ample space all round it you will be better disposed to listen. The smaller the seed the shallower it should be sown, and it is better to sprinkle some fine soil over your sowings than to attempt to rake them in, a method which usually results in an uneven distribution. Look out for slugs. Put twiggy sticks among those seedlings that will eventually grow tall enough to need staking.

In a short article like this it is impossible to give an exhaustive list, but I might single out a few annuals that are less commonly grown than the usual clarkias, godetias, and so on. To take one of the tiniest first, I am very fond of *Leptosiphon*; only three inches in height, but very varied in colour, it is charming as an edging, or among stones, or in paving. It likes full sun. *Linaria* associates well with it, being several inches taller, but of the same delicate character, as the name *Fairy Bouquet* will suggest. *Phacelia campanularia*, nine inches, sown in large patches, will quickly make a mat of gentian-blue.

Among the stronger colours, *Coreopsis Crimson King* is

a brilliant bronze dwarf. *Dimorphotheca aurantiaca*, the orange South African daisy, looks like a patch of sunlight on the ground (but shuts itself up when the sun goes in); and among the calendulas there is a strain called by the repulsive name of *Art Shades*, which throws a variety of pretty colours in apricot, buff, and straw, less violent than the old *Orange King*. A study of a seedsman's catalogue will give many suggestions, and there is also a very useful book, *Annuals* by Roy Hay, published by the Bodley Head at 12s. 6d.

May

May 1948

By the time this article appears the lilac should be in flower. It is not called lilac now by the experts: it is called syringa; and what we used to call syringa is now called philadelphus. All very confusing, so let us incorrectly retain the old names for the moment, when everyone will know what I mean.

Lilac (or laylock, if you prefer) is one of the few old favourites which has been definitely improved in recent years. Frankly, the pale mauve type was a washy thing. The newer sorts have gained in colour, size, and scent. I suppose that everyone is by now familiar with the earlier improvements: *Souvenir de Louis Spath*, and *Charles Joly*, both dark red; or *Charles X*, deep purple; or *Madame Lemoine*, double white; none of which is easy to beat. But not everyone, I find, is familiar with the more recent hybrids, carrying truly noble plumes of immense weight: *Réaumur*, dark red; *President Poincaré* and *Pasteur*, both claret; *Congo*, very dark reddish-purple; *Jeanne d'Arc*, double white; *Mme F. Morel*, mauvish pink; *Maréchal Foch*, red.

Any lilac is 'easy': they do not object to lime, in fact they like it; they need no pruning, though it is most advantageous to cut off the faded flowers, *this is really*

33

important; they are perfectly hardy; and very long-lived unless they suddenly die back, which sometimes happens. Few plants could give you more for 8s. 6d. or half a guinea. Of course they repay rich cultivation; most plants do. And they like the sun.

The old syringa or Mock Orange, is another easy-going shrub, too often forgotten. Personally I like the early, very sweet-scented species, called *coronarius*, found in most old gardens; but *Virginal*, with double flowers, is a lovely cool green-and-white sight in midsummer; and so are *Belle Etoile* and *purpureo-maculatus*, both blotched with maroon in the centre. *Grandiflorus* is the one with big single white flowers, very decorative but entirely scent-less, which may be a recommendation for people who do not like heavily-scented flowers in their rooms. By the way, if you strip all the leaves from cut branches of syringa they will last far longer, besides gaining in beauty. Try. And smash the woody stems with a hammer.

I end with a counsel and with a warning. *Counsel:* try to see plants in bloom during the coming months, either in private gardens open to the public – and there are many, my own garden, for instance, is open every day until the end of October – or at shows, or in nursery gardens, or in gardens such as Kew and the Royal Horticultural Society's place at Wisley. There is no better way of judging what plants really look like and what really appeals to you. *Warning:* this applies to slug-bait. Whatever you use, keep it away from dogs and cats, either by mixing it with tea-leaves or by tilting something like a tile or a piece of glass over it. It is wise to be on the safe side.

May 9, 1948

Agreeable incidents do continue to occur from time to time, even in 1948; and there still seem to be days when things marvellously go right instead of wrong, rarities to be recorded with gratitude before they can be forgotten.

Such a day, culminating in such an incident, was given to me recently. I had had occasion to drive across ten miles of Kent, through the orchard country. The apple-blossom was not yet fully out; and it was still in that fugitive precious stage of being more of a promise than a fulfilment. Apple-blossom too quickly becomes over-blown, whereas its true character is to be as tightly youthful as an eighteen-year-old poet. There they were, the closed buds just flushing pink, making a faintly roseate haze over the old trees grey with age; closed buds of youth graciously blushing as youth must blush in the presence of age, knowing very well that within a few months they themselves would turn into the apples of autumnal fruit.

But if the apple-blossom was no more than a pink veil thrown over the orchards, the cherry was at its most magnificent. Never had it looked more lavish than this year (1948), nor so white, so candidly white. This heavy whiteness of the cherry, always enhanced by the contrasting blackness of the branches, was on this particular afternoon deepened – if white may be said to deepen – by a pewter-grey sky of storm as a backcloth; and I thought, not for the first time, how perfectly married were these two effects of April: the dazzling blossom and the peculiarly lurid heaven which is only half a menace. Only half, for however wrathful it may pretend to be overhead, there are gleams of light round the edges, with lances of sun striking a church tower somewhere in the landscape. It is not a true threat; it is a temporary threat, put on for its theatrical effect – Nature's original of that most strange and beautiful of man's new inventions, flood-lighting.

Enriched by these experiences I came home, expecting no further delight that day; but on arrival I saw a closed van at the front door. Having long awaited some spare parts to repair the boiler, dreary, yet necessary, I walked round to the back of the van, thinking how quickly utilitarian life returned to oust beauty, and with a sigh prepared to investigate some graceless assortment of ironmongery whose function would be incomprehensible to me. But there was no such thing. Instead, a smiling young man confronted me, saying he did not know if I would be interested, but he had brought these . . . and opened the van as he spoke.

'These' were giant pansies, thousands and thousands of them. The van's dark interior was a cavern of colour. Some royal hand had flung rugs of velvet over the stacks of wooden trays. Purples were there; and subtler colours than purple: bronze and greenish-yellow and claret and rose-red, all in their queer cat-faces of crumpled velvet. I stood amazed. What an imaginative young man, I thought, to hawk this giant strain round the countryside, selling his plants to any buyer. When I questioned him, he said, modestly, that he hoped people would not be able to resist them.

He was probably right, and I wish him good luck in his enterprise. As for those whose houses do not lie on his road, a packet of seed should serve the purpose, and by next spring the ground should appear as though spread with the most sumptuous carpet from Isfahan.

May 29, 1949

In these somewhat scrappy notes I go, rightly or wrongly, on the assumption that my readers welcome suggestions for something which, though not difficult to grow, is a little out of the ordinary. This week I would therefore like to put in a plea for some tulips less usually seen than our old friends the Cottage or the Darwin. I know full well that tulips will be over by the time these words appear in print, but as all good gardeners keep a notebook for their autumn orders months ahead, I put forward these hints for your autumn list.

The Parrot or Dragon tulips are well named, for some of them really do suggest the more gaudy macaws in their colouring, and the jagged edges of their petals always remind me of the wyvern, that winged heraldic cousin of the dragon. I tried this comparison on a gardening friend, who stared at me blankly and said she couldn't think what I meant, and what was a wyvern anyhow? But still I think that one should look at flowers in an imaginative way, to squeeze the fullest enjoyment from them.

The pink *Fantasy*, with its apple-green feathering, is fairly common; *Red Champion* is a deeper version of

Fantasy, a real cherry-red, opening to an enormous size, and heavily fringed; *Orange Favourite*, smudged with buttercup yellow and green, not quite so large; the *Blue Parrot*, which is not blue at all but a deep mauve, really the colour of blackberry fool (horticulturists sometimes have very queer ideas about naming colours); *Sunshine*, a golden yellow – all these are fun to grow, and no more expensive to buy than the ordinary tulip.

But there are other far more frenzied variations. *Gadelan* was the maddest-looking tulip I ever had in my garden. It was smeared with as many colours as a painter's palette after a good day's work – dark blue, dark red, purple, green, white – and as to size, it must have measured eight inches across when fully opened. This costs 1s. 3d. a bulb, so I got only three as an experiment, and abstained altogether from the *Black Parrot* at a guinea. *Gadelan* was enough, for the moment, to keep me satisfied and startled.

'Parrotting,' as it is called, is due to genetic change, i.e. a kind of sporting. It is not a disease.

May 7, 1950

Perhaps I should entitle this article 'In Your House', or 'Your Garden in Your House', because I want to write something about cut flowers, inspired by an interesting letter from a gentleman describing himself as a botanist and horticulturist who has carried out researches on this very subject. This is the time of the year when owners of gardens begin to pick more recklessly, with less dread

of spoiling their outdoor show, but this pleasurable occu-
pation does take a long time, and the busy woman wants
to make her flowers last as long as possible.

'The cause of difficulties with cut flowers,' says my
correspondent, 'lies in the entry of air into the water-
tubes of the flower stems during the period between
cutting the flowers and placing them in water.' To prevent such disappointment, he recommends that you
should place your newly cut flowers in recently boiled
water while it is still just above tepid, i.e. not hot enough
to sting your hand but warm enough to give your fingers
an agreeable sensation of warmth. Cut your flowers, he
says, during dull, sunless hours; a recommendation that
we have all found out for ourselves; but I wonder how
many readers of this article are going to go wandering
round with a kettle of recently boiled water? These
things take time, and one has other things to do. Still,
I shall try it.

My correspondent condemns as an old wives' tale the
placing of aspirin tablets or copper coins in the water.
He gives a slight approval to lumps of charcoal, in so far
as they absorb air from the water. I suppose that we all
have our theories, but this idea of air entering the stems
is worth consideration. I pass it on to you.

I now return to the garden proper. Have you got *Viburnum Carlcephalum*? If not, please get it at once. It is a
hybrid of *Viburnum Carlesii*, which we all know and grow,
and it is a far better thing. Its head of flower is tighter
and denser; its scent is stronger; and its habit is vigorous.
My own plant is young and small; but I am told by

people who have seen it growing fully developed that it makes a huge bush in course of time. It is one of the most exciting things I have grown for years past; not very exciting as to its colour, which is white flushed with pink in the bud, but most exciting as to its powerful scent.

It is flowering now, April–May, and is obtainable from Messrs. John Scott, The Royal Nurseries, Merriott, Somerset.

Halesia carolina, the snowdrop tree, is also just coming into flower. This is a very pretty flowering tree, seldom seen; it is hung with white, bell-shaped blossoms, among pale green leaves, all along the branches. It can be grown as a bush in the open, or trained against a wall. There is a better version of it called *Halesia monticola*, but if you cannot obtain this from your nurseryman *Halesia carolina* will do as well. Messrs. Hillier, of Winchester, however, list them both.

May 28, 1950

The roses are coming out, and I hope everybody will take the opportunity of seeing as many of the *old* roses as possible. They may roughly be described as roses which should be grown as shrubs; that is, allowed to ramp away into big bushes, and allowed also to travel about underground if they are on their own roots and come up in fine carelessness some yards from the parent plant. It is impossible in so short an article to give an adequate list, and even more impossible to indicate their charm, usefulness, and beauty, but there are gardens in which they may be seen and nurserymen from whom they may be obtained. (One garden where a large collection may be seen is Hidcote Manor, in Gloucestershire, near Broadway and Chipping Campden; for times of opening, which are several days a week, consult the National Trust, 42 Queen Anne's Gate, London, SW1.) I put this in for the benefit of readers who live in that part of the country; and must add that, apart from its old roses, it is, perhaps, the loveliest garden in the west of England.)

The old roses are a wide subject to embark on. You have to consider the Gallicas, the Damasks, the Centifolias or Cabbage, the Musks, the China, the Rose of Provins . . . all more romantic the one than the other. Take this phrase alone: 'In the twelfth century the dark red Gallic rose was cultivated by the Arabs in Spain with the tradition that it was brought from Persia in the seventh century.' That is pure poetry, surely, although it comes from a serious article in a serious journal and was not intended as anything but a mere statement of fact. It should send us with a new zest in pursuit of these once neglected beauties.

They are not neglected now; their virtues are recognized by professional gardeners and amateur gardeners alike. True, I have heard conventionally minded people remark that they like a rose to be a rose, by which they apparently mean an overblown pink, scarlet, or yellow object, desirable enough in itself, but lacking the subtlety to be found in some of these traditional roses which might well be picked off a medieval tapestry or a piece of

Stuart needlework. Indeed, I think you should approach them as though they were textiles rather than flowers. The velvet vermilion of petals, the stamens of quivering gold, the slaty purple of *Cardinal Richelieu*, the loose dark red and gold of *Alain Blanchard*; I could go on for ever, but always I should come back to the idea of embroidery and of velvet and of the damask with which some of them share their name. They have a quality of their own; and from the gardener's point of view they give little trouble. No pruning to speak of, only a yearly removal of dead wood, and some strong stakes which seldom need renewing.

Have I pleaded in vain?

June

June 15, 1947

In a recent article I referred briefly to the fact that many privately-owned gardens are now regularly thrown open to the public, and as this remark appears to have aroused some interest, I thought I might take this opportunity of amplifying it. I made it in a desire to urge keen gardeners to see as many gardens as possible, for the sake of the practical hints they might pick up there, apart from the pleasure they might gain. Nothing could be more useful to the amateur gardener than to observe other people's ideas, other people's successes, and other people's failures. At flower shows, such as the Chelsea Show, one knows that every plant has been specially grown, richly fed, and luxuriously prepared for the great moment, thus arousing our suspicion that its grower has sat up with it night after night, holding an umbrella over it when too heavy a thunder-shower threatened its petals; ready with a hot-water bottle lest a late frost should come with a cold breath; and in many ways cosseting it for the supreme peak of its life when it must be exposed to the gaze of the King and Queen and all the Royal Family at a morning preview, and then to the expert criticism of Fellows of the Royal Horticultural Society during the afternoon. A plant in a garden is different from this: it has had to take its chance. It has been ordinarily grown. It has suffered from our common climate even as we all have to suffer. Seeing it grow in somebody else's garden, we can assess its normal performance; we can then decide whether we ourselves like it and whether we dare to attempt it or not.

These gardens now open to our wandering inspection are widespread and various. They range over all the counties of England, Scotland, and Wales. I have been looking through the England and Wales list, which runs so generously into seventy pages. What enticements are therein offered! Who could resist the desire to penetrate without delay into precincts with such romantic names as Hutton John, Heronden Eastry, Nether Lypiatt, Bevington Lordship, St John Jerusalem, Castle Drogo, The House in the Wood, or Flower Lilies? All poetry is there, suggestive and evocative. One could go and sit in those gardens on a summer evening, and imagine what one's own garden (and one's life) might be. And again, who could fail to respond to the magic of an invitation to 'Magna Carta Island, until dusk,' or to a garden mysteriously named The Isle of Thorns?

Nor is this all. At Tinker's Corner, for instance, you are offered tea *and music*; Bickleigh Castle provides flood-lighting and a moated Saxon chapel, modestly adding '*romantic interest*', which one can well believe. Little Whyley Hall somewhat startlingly tenders not only cups of tea but big-game herds. You can see Shelley's birthplace and Rudyard Kipling's house. You will be given 'strawberries if ripe' at Kempsons in June. At Old Westwell you can see fur rabbits; peach blossom, topiary, and rare shrubs are elsewhere suggested for your enjoyment. And if you like to see how Royalty lives, you can go to Sandringham on any Wednesday during June, July, and September.

These are no more than random pickings out of an immense bran-pie. Anyone who wants the complete list can get it from the Organizing Secretary, National Gardens Scheme, 57 Lower Belgrave Street, SW1, telephone Sloane 9948. You pay a shilling entrance fee, and all benefit goes to the Queen's Institute of District Nursing. (*Note:* I should add that since this article appeared, the Queen's Institute has come to an arrangement with the National Trust, by which a percentage of the takings are given to the National Trust towards the cost of such gardens as are the property of the Trust.)

June 26, 1949

I am no blind believer in the 'improved' modern flower: I don't like delphiniums with stalks like tree-trunks; I don't like roses with no scent and a miserable constitution; but for the Russell lupins and the bearded irises one must make an exception. Everyone knows, and grows, the lupins; not everyone, I think, has yet realized the extreme beauty of the irises. So as June is just the moment to see them in flower I thought I would remind you of their beauty and their many advantages.

Their beauty is beyond dispute. No velvet can rival the richness of their falls; or, let us say, it is to velvet only that we may compare them. That is surely enough to claim for any flower? They suggest velvet, pansies, wine – anything you like, that possesses texture as well as colour. (Wine, to a connoisseur, does possess texture.) Then, as to their advantages, they are the easiest plants to grow. All they ask is a well-drained, sunny place so that their rhizomes may get the best possible baking; a scatter of lime in autumn or in spring; and division every third year.

It may sound tiresome and laborious to dig up and divide plants every third year, but in the case of the iris it is a positive pleasure. It means that they increase so rapidly. Relatively expensive to buy in the first instance, by the end of the second or third year you have so large a clump from a single rhizome that you can break them up, spread them out, and even give them away. The best time to do this is immediately after they have finished flowering – in other words, at the end of June or beginning of July. Do not bury the rhizome, but leave it showing above the ground; this, again, is in order to let the sun reach it. The plant knows this, however, and will push itself up even if you do cover it over; but why give it that extra bit of trouble, when it already has a great deal to do?

Colours must, of course, be left to the individual taste. Those which we may roughly call reddish include *Cresset*, *Senlac*, *Mrs Valerie West*, *Maréchal Ney*, *Red Rover* and *Cheerio*, which has nothing wrong with it except its name. The wine-coloured ones include the magnificent *Betelgeuse*, *Melchior* and *Ambassador*. *Cinnabar* is a rich pansy-purple, very tall. All of these range in price from 1s. 6d. to 3s. 6d. There are also many fine yellows; but the best thing is to obtain a catalogue from a nursery that specializes in irises, say Messers. Wallace, Tunbridge Wells; or the Orpington Nursery, Orpington, Kent. The descriptions are not misleading, for no adjective could be too extravagant. It is only you that will be.

June 4, 1950

I have a gardening dodge which I find very useful. It concerns colour-schemes and plant-groupings. You know how quickly one forgets what one's garden has looked like during different weeks progressively throughout the year? One makes a mental note, or even a written note, and then the season changes and one forgets what one meant at the time. One has written 'Plant something yellow near the yellow tulips', or 'Plant something tall behind the lupins', and then autumn comes and plants have died down, and one scratches one's head trying to remember what on earth one intended by that.

My system is more practical. I observe, for instance, a great pink, lacy crinoline of the May-flowering tamarisk, of which I put in two snippets years ago, and which now spreads the exuberance of its petticoats twenty feet wide over a neglected corner of the garden. What could I plant near it to enhance its colour? It must, of course, be something which will flower at the same time. So I try effects, picking flowers elsewhere, rather in the way that one makes a flower arrangement in the house, sticking them into the ground and then standing back to observe the harmony. The dusky, rosy *Iris Senlac* is just the right colour: I must split up my clumps as soon as they have finished flowering and make a group of those near the tamarisk for next May. The common pink columbine, almost a weed, would do well for under-planting, or some pink pansies, *Crimson Queen*, or the wine-red shades, as a carpet; and, for something really noble, the giant fox-tail lily, *Eremurus robustus*, eight to ten feet high. I cut, with reluctance, one precious spike from a distant group, and stick it in; it looks fine, like a cathedral spire flushed warm in the sunset. Undoubtedly I should have some *eremuri* next year with the plumy curtains of the tamarisk behind them, but the *eremuri* are too expensive and one cannot afford many of them.

This is just one example. One has the illusion of being an artist painting a picture – putting in a dash of colour here, taking out another dash of colour there, until the whole composition is to one's liking, and at least one knows exactly what effect will be produced twelve months hence.

To conclude, may I recommend planting tamarisk? It is graceful, hardy, and no bother. You can control its size by hard pruning, if necessary, though for my own part I like to see it growing free. *T. pentandra*, sometimes called *T. hispidi aestivalis*, flowers in August and September; *T. tetrandra* is the one I have been writing about, and flowers in May. *T. anglica* flowers in late summer and does particularly well by the sea, where it can be used as a windbreak. They all strike easily from cuttings in autumn.

June 18, 1950

Two years ago I had what I thought might be a bright idea. It has turned out so bright, in both senses of the word, that I must pass it on.

I had two small windswept beds (the size was eight yards long by five yards wide each), divided by a path of paving stones down the middle. I tried every sort of thing in them, including a mad venture of hollyhocks, which, of course, got flattened by the prevailing south-west wind, however strongly we staked them. So then I decided I must have something very low growing, which would not suffer from the wind, and scrapped the hollyhocks, and dibbled in lots and lots of thyme, and now have a sort of lawn which, while it is densely flowering in purple and red, looks like a Persian carpet laid flat on the ground out of doors. The bees think that I have laid it for their especial benefit. It really is a lovely sight; I do not want to boast, but I cannot help being pleased with it; it is so seldom that one's experiments in gardening are wholly successful.

The thyme we used was the cultivated or garden form of the wild thyme, *Thymus serpyllum*, the form you see creeping about between paving-stones on paths and terraces. *Serpyllum* comes from the Latin *serpere*, to creep; think of serpent; and in fact two old English names for the wild thyme were serpille and serpolet. My serpolet lawn. . . . The Romans believed its fragrance to be a remedy for melancholia; and in later years, our own Elizabethan times, it was thought to cure sciatica and whooping cough, headache, phrenzy, and lethargy.

We had the common purple sort, and the sort called *coccineus* to give the redder patches, and also a little of the white, which varied the pattern.

I have planted a few bulbs of small things in amongst the thyme, to give some interest in the spring, when the thyme is merely green. A patch of crocuses; a patch of the miniature narcissus; a patch of the little pink cyclamen. It occurs to me also that if you have not a flat bed to devote to a thyme-lawn you could fill a sunny bank with it. Steep grass banks are always awkward to mow, but the thyme would not need any mowing, and it should revel in a sunny exposure with the good drainage of a slope. You might plant some of the rock-roses, or sun-roses, hybrids of *Helianthemum vulgare*, amongst the thyme on a bank, though I would not do so in a thyme-lawn, where it would spoil the effect of flatness. These sun-roses can be obtained in a variety of brilliant colours, ranging from pale buff and yellow to tomato pink and deep red, and they flower for at least six weeks during May and June.

I know I get too easily carried away by some new enthusiasm and by the ideas it suggests; but that is half the fun of gardening. I will not apologize too humbly; so, instead of boasting, I will make two practical recommendations as an end to this article. First, do plant *Abelia triflora*. It flowers in June, grows to the size of what we used to call Syringa, and is smothered in white, funnel-shaped flowers with the strongest scent of Jasmine. Second, do plant *Cytisus Battandieri*. This is a broom; and when it has grown into a large tree it is hung with gold-yellow tassels in June, with a peculiar scent. I could not think what the scent was, till my kind host who had it growing in his garden fixed it for me: 'It is the scent of pineapple mixed with fruit salad.' He was right.

Cytisus Battandieri is supposed to be hardy, but I suspect that in cold districts it would be safer to train it against a wall.

July

July 20, 1947

This is a good moment to think of your future stock. Plants, and even seeds, are expensive to buy, but by raising your own nursery you can get plants by the thousand if you wish, for no cost beyond your own time and labour. It is well worth saving the seeds of annuals, biennials, and even perennials, either from your own garden or the gardens of friends who may have better varieties than you have. They must be quite ripe, and can be stored in little air-tight tins, such as the tins that typewriter ribbons come in, and sown in September when they will have time to make sturdy growth before the winter. Pansies, Indian pinks, columbines, foxglove, forget-me-not, primrose, polyanthus, anemones, lupins, and many other garden flowers can be thus harvested. Sow them thinly in drills on a finely pulverized seed-bed, and move them to their flowering quarters in the spring.

Remember that home-saved seeds will not necessarily come true, as the insects will have interfered with them. All the same, it is worth trying, and you might even get an interesting hybrid.

If you feel more ambitious you will be well advised to buy some packets of the improved varieties from a regular seedsman. Messrs. Sutton, of Reading, have some fine columbines. *Crimson Star, Scarlet and Gold, Longissima*, a magnificiently long-spurred yellow, and *Azure Fairy*, a really lovely pale blue, will all surprise you if you have hitherto grown only the old-fashioned kinds. The results of a pinch of seed from the grand new delphiniums (obtainable from Messrs. Blackmore and Langdon of Bath), if you can't cadge some from a friend, will put you out of conceit with the sorts that have hitherto contented you. Seeds of the hybrid *Alstroemeria*, or Peruvian lily, will germinate freely, but as they are rather tricky to transplant, I should advise you to sow them direct where you want them eventually to grow; they like good drainage and full sun, and the *Ligtu hybrids*, pink or buff-coloured, are the sort to ask for; or *Alstroemeria haemantha* if you want a flaming orange one. Cover the seedlings with bracken, or with the twiggy tops of old pea-sticks if you haven't any bracken, for the first winter of their young life.

Lilies may also be raised from seed, instead of paying half a crown or more for a single bulb. *Lilium regale* will come up as thick as mustard and cress by this method; you will have to wait two or possibly three years before the bulbs come to flowering size, but think of the economy and of the staggered crop that you can raise, if you sow even one little row of seed every year.

Clematis will grow from seed, and so will broom; but as both these hate being disturbed it is advisable to grow them single in small pots, when they can be tipped out without noticing that anything has happened.

Cuttings of many flowering shrubs such as ceanothus, can be taken in July. Set them very firmly in a drill filled with sharp sand, in the open in the shade. As with rose cuttings, you should put in more than you need. A closed frame or even a hand-light put over cuttings for the first ten days or so will help them to strike, but they will give quite good results without this.

July 10, 1949

One learns a lot from visiting other people's gardens. One gets ideas. I got a lot of ideas from a famous garden I visited recently; so many, that I feel like a wine-glass spilling over; so many, that I cannot compress them all into this short article. So in this article I will concentrate only on the hedges I saw in that famous garden.

Hedges are always an important feature in any garden, however small, however large. Hedges are the things that cut off one section of the garden from another; they play an essential part in the general design. The only question is: What shall we plant for our hedges?

In this article I shall disregard the question of the flowering hedges; that is another subject, to which I hope to revert later on. I am here concerned only with the solid, useful hedge, deciduous or evergreen. We don't show nearly enough imagination about these. We still stick to such dull things as privet or *Lonicera nitida*, not realizing that we can make a muddle-of-a-hedge, which has a solidity and a character of its own.

In that famous garden I saw many different kinds of hedge, all planted in an imaginative mixture. There was yew mixed with box, and yew mixed with holly, and holly mixed with copper beech, and hornbeam mixed with ordinary beech, and one hedge mixed with five different sorts of plants in it – beech, holly, yew, box, and horn-beam, I think they were – but the most surprisingly sumptuous hedge, to my mind, was one made entirely of the copper beech.

We all know the copper beech as a tree; but few of us have thought of growing it as a hedge. Grown as a tree it has now acquired suburban associations. It works in with such things as *Prunus Pissardii*, very pretty in their way, but with which we are now only too familiar. Grown as a hedge, the copper beech acquires a completely different character. You would not believe the richness of its colouring. It has purple tinges in the depths of it, a sort of mulberry purple, and then Venetian red; and then the tips of the young shoots so bright a ruby as they catch the sunlight – oh, why, I cried to myself, don't we all plant even a short length of copper beech hedge? For my own part, I am certainly going to.

July 2, 1950

There are some moments when I feel pleased with my garden, and other moments when I despair. The pleased moments usually happen in spring, and last up to the middle of June. By that time all the freshness has gone off; everything has become heavy; everything has lost that adolescent look, that look of astonishment at its own youth. The middle-aged spread has begun.

It is then that the *Alstroemerias* come into their own.

Lumps of colour . . . I have mentioned them before, I know, but a reminder will do no harm. They are in flower now, so this is the opportunity to go and see them, either in a local nurseryman's plot, or in a private garden, or at a flower show. The yellow Peruvian lily, *A. aurantiaca*, was and is a common sight in cottage gardens and old herbaceous borders, where it was regarded almost as a weed, but it has been superseded by the far more beautiful *Ligtu* hybrids, in varied colours of coral and buff, and by *A. haemantha*, a brilliant orange. (Keep the orange away from the coral, for they do not mix well together, and whoever it was who said Nature made no mistakes in colour-harmony was either colour-blind or a sentimentalist. Nature sometimes makes the most hideous mistakes; and it is up to us gardeners to control and correct them.)

The *Ligtu* hybrids of *Alstroemeria*, and also the orange *A. haemantha*, can and should be grown from seed. You sow the seed in February or March, where you intend the plant to grow and flower. I am sure I am right in recommending this method. One reason is that the seed germinates very freely; another reason is that the roots of *Alstroemeria* are extremely brittle, and thus are difficult to transplant; and the third reason is that plants are expensive to buy and may fail owing to the difficulty of transplantation. Therefore I say sow your own seed and wait for two years before your clumps come to their fulfilment.

You could also sow one or two seeds in a pot, in those cardboard pots which dissolve after they have been dropped into the ground – this is perhaps the ideal method.

They demand full sun and good drainage, by which I mean that they would not like any shade or a water-logged soil. They are sun-lovers. They also demand staking, not stiff staking, but a support of twiggy branches to hold them up; otherwise they flop and snap and lose their beauty, lying flat after a thunderstorm of rain or a sudden gale, such as we get from time to time in our usually temperate country. This is a counsel of caution. Prop up your *Alstroemerias*, if you take my advice to grow them, by twiggy pea-sticks.

They are the perfect flower for cutting, lasting weeks in water in the house.

The seedlings would like a little protection in winter if there is a hard frost. Some bracken will do, scattered over them. Once established, they are hardy enough to withstand anything but a particularly bad winter. It is only the young that are tender, needing a little love and care.

August

August 17, 1947

I write this note far from home, on a not unenviable expedition which involves wandering round other people's gardens. Most of them are still suffering from the neglect of the war years, from shortage of labour, and probably also shortage of funds, and only in a few cases the prosperity of herbaceous borders still flaunted under the long old walls. Such luxuries are not for the majority, so I turned to consider the flowering shrubs, those permanent mainstays which increase in value with every year, and demand less attention than any other plant in the garden.

It is generally recognized that the late summer shrubs are far less numerous than those of spring; nevertheless, some were prominent.

In some gardens the hydrangeas were making a great display, but they look their best in large clumps, I think, not as the single specimens for which a small garden has only room; and in any case they always remind me of coloured wigs, so I really prefer the looser kinds called *paniculata*, which have a flat central head fringed by open sterile flowers; a particularly pleasing variety is called *Sargentii*.

Among the brilliant climbers, *Bignonia grandiflora* with

red-orange trumpets was as startling as the humble nasturtium in colour, but far more graceful and much taller in habit. It should never be planted against red brick, but against grey stone or against a white-washed cottage it looks both gay and splendid. (Nurserymen sometimes sell it under the name *Tecoma* or *Campsis radicans*.) The best variety is *Campsis Mme Galen*. Another orange climber, not quite so showy, goes by the unfortunate name of *Eccremocarpus scaber*; if I knew the English name for it, I would tell you. Perhaps it hasn't one. Not always considered quite hardy, it came through last winter unharmed. I notice also that that very lovely small flowering tree of white and gold, *Eucryphia intermedia*, has survived the winter; it is rather slow of growth, but all patient gardeners should plant at least one or two. It has the advantage of flowering while still quite young, in August just when such a stop-gap is most needed.

A reminder: bulbs for flowering in bowls next winter should now be planted in fibre, and kept in the dark till their little bleached noses show a couple of inches high. If a dark cupboard is not available, take the hint of a friend of mine who grew them most successfully under the sitting-room sofa.

August 7, 1949

It is not often that I mention vegetables, but I should like to put in a good word for the Globe artichoke. It appears to be almost unknown in this country. An enterprising greengrocer told me that he bought some in the market but had been obliged to throw them out, unsold, on to the rubbish heap. Yet there must surely be something to be said for a vegetable which is grown by the acre in such gastronomic countries as France and Italy.

There are three different kinds of artichoke: the Jerusalem, the Chinese, and the Globe. The Jerusalem, probably the best known in England, is a tuber and is a most insipid vegetable on which no epicure should waste time or space. (It has no connection with Jerusalem, by the way: the name is a corruption of *girasole*, turning-with-the-sun, the Italian for sunflower, to which the Jerusalem artichoke is botanically related.) The Chinese, also a tuber, is seldom met with but highly to be recommended. It is like a little whorled seashell to look at, and is very useful in winter when vegetables are scarce. Plant the tubers in rows in March; do not allow the plants to get too dry in summer; lift the tubers in November, and store in sand, using them as you require. Boil them first, and then fry them in a little butter.

But it is the Globe artichoke I really want to plead for. This is not a tuber, but a tall and extremely handsome plant with deeply indented grey-green leaves which are most decorative in the garden and splendid in a big vase of summer flowers; they have a sculptural, architectural quality, like the leaves of acanthus, which gives dignity to the gay, mixed bunch. It thus serves a double purpose, for even if you decide not to use it as a vegetable it can still be grown for its foliage and for the thistle-like purple heads which it will produce if allowed to flower. These, however are the heads you ought to eat before they reach the flowering stage; and do eat them *young*, I beseech you, before they have had time to grow old and tough. There are many ways in which they can be cooked; you can either boil them, whole, in salted water for twenty to thirty minutes and then eat them hot or cold, with melted butter or oil and vinegar respectively; or divest them of their leaves, using only the bottom – what the French call *fonds d'artichaut* – in a variety of dishes, as an entrée with half a tomato sitting on top, or as a savoury with cheese sauce, or stuffed *à la Barigoule* . . . but this is not a cookery book, and any good recipe book will give you ideas. An old tradition, on which I was brought up, says that after eating an artichoke you should drink a glass of cold water to bring out the flavour.

The Globe artichoke admittedly takes up a good deal of room: at least three feet wide and six feet tall, it may seem out of proportion in a small kitchen garden, but, as I have suggested, it may be given a place in the flower garden for its decorative value alone. It likes full sun, and it should be planted in April. It is reasonably hardy, but to be on the safe side you might cover it with some litter, or bracken, or ashes, during the winter months or especially if you foresee late frosts in May when the young shoots are coming up. I have never bothered to do this, and my artichokes have come safely through some very hard winters, but I pass on the advice for what it is worth. The gardening books, also, will tell you to renew your plants every three years. They may be right. All I can say is that my own plants have been in my garden for over twelve years and show no sign of going off; they crop as well as ever and have received little attention, so on this point I must disagree with the gardening books. Practical experience is worth more than many pages of print.

For the comfort of northern readers, I find that an old book printed in 1832 records that 'Nowhere does the artichoke arrive at greater perfection than in the Orkney Islands.'

August 13, 1950

I revert to the subject of hedges, since they are so important in a garden, large or small; and, moreover, now that many people are moving into new houses with a plot of land demanding enclosure, the question of hedges becomes urgent: what to plant and when to plant it. Generally speaking, early autumn is the best time, and let us remember always that money spent on a good hedge is money well invested, for year by year it gives an increasingly good return.

Our American friends do not like hedges. They do not share our love of privacy, and maintain that if you plant a hedge round your garden you are doing something undemocratic and may even have 'something to hide.' Fortunately for us and for the beauty of our country we suffer from no such notions. We might well, however, display a little more imagination in our choice of hedging plants, instead of sticking with such depressing fidelity to privet, quick, *Lonicera nitida*, and *cupressus macrocarpa*.

There are two kinds of hedge, the useful and the

ornamental. The useful hedge has the job of keeping animals out, and thus offers less scope for decorative informality, but life even in the country is not invariably a battle against cows or goats, and there are many plants which will afford charm and colour as well as providing the necessary line of demarcation. Rose hedges, for example, promise to become increasingly popular, and what could be lovelier than, say, a long stretch of some Hybrid Musk or sweet-scented Rugosa? Again, I can imagine such evergreen flowering shrubs as *Osmanthus Delavayi* or *Choisya ternata*, or the silver-leaved *Elæagnus macrophylla*, or the many-coloured cydonias – incorrectly called japonicas – or the many varieties of escallonia, especially valuable near the sea. It would be impossible to give anything approaching a complete list of suggestions here; but a most practical little book has just come out, at the moderate price of 1s. 6d.: *Better Hedges*, by Roy Hay, obtainable from Roy Hay Publications, Dolphin Cottage, Grayswood, Haslemere. Illustrated by photographs, it tells you how to plant; how to cultivate; how to cut; how to renovate; and, most valuable of all, ends up with eleven pages of special lists. These include hedge plants for small gardens; plants for formal or informal hedges; plants for the seaside, for semi-shade, for light soils, for heavy soils, for chalky soils; and some good hedge-plants for various situations and purposes, with brief descriptions and instructions how to prune, trim and clip. There is also a note on hedge-cutting with labour-saving machinery.

August 20, 1950

At this time of the year, this dull time, this heavy August time, when everything has lost its youth and is over-grown and mature, the Japanese anemones come into flower with a queer reminder of spring. They manage, in late summer, to suggest the lightness of spring flowers. Tall, bold, stiff, they come up every year, and may indeed be regarded as a weed in the garden, so luxuriantly do they grow and increase.

The common white anemone *Japonica alba* is the one best known to us all. It is a most accommodating plant in many ways, because it does not resent being grown in half shade and is not particular as to soil. Neither does it require staking. It has a stiff resistant stalk. The only thing it resents is being moved. It takes at least two seasons to recover from removal; but when those two seasons have gone by, it will give you a rich return in white flowers with golden centres and a very long flowering period as bud after bud comes out. This alone makes it a satisfactory plant to grow in a shady or neglected corner where few other herbaceous plants would consent to flourish; but there are other varieties besides the common white, and it is to these that I would like to draw your attention.

The pale mauve one is, I suppose, almost as well known as the common white. It is very pretty, a lilac-mauve; but there are others, such as the variety called *Prince Henry*, a really deep mauve-pink, growing to a height of three to four feet and flowering from August

to September. This will cost you 1s. 6d. a plant and is
well worth it. There are also shorter ones, growing only
to one or two feet, such as *Mont Rose*, which is described
as old rose in colour, and *Profusion*, purplish-red, two
feet high. I must confess that I have not grown *Mont Rose*
or *Profusion* and know them only by repute; but *Prince
Henry* grows in my garden, in a fortunate accidental
association under the wine-coloured clematis *Kermesina*.
This late-flowering clematis, belonging to the Viticella
group of clematis, should be more often planted. It
produces a mass of its small wine-coloured flowers, like
a Burgundy wine held up to the light, at the very same
time as the Japanese anemone *Prince Henry* comes to its
best. They match one another to perfection.

My only grievance against the Japanese anemone is
that it tires and droops once cut, and thus is no good
for picking. But in the garden, however, it comes as a
salvation in this dreary, uninteresting time of the year.

September

September 29, 1946

The two great planting months, October and November, are close upon us, and those gardeners who desire the maximum of reward with the minimum of labour would be well advised to concentrate upon the flowering shrubs and flowering trees. How deeply I regret that fifteen years ago, when I was forming my own garden, I did not plant these desirable objects in sufficient quantity. They would by now be large adults instead of the scrubby, spindly infants I contemplate with impatience as the seasons come round.

That error is one from which I would wish to save my fellow-gardeners, so, taking this opportunity, I implore them to secure trees and bushes from whatever nurseryman can supply them: they will give far less trouble than the orthodox herbaceous flower, they will demand no annual division, many of them will require no pruning; in fact, all that many of them will ask of you is to watch them grow yearly into a greater splendour, and what more could be exacted of any plant?

Your choice will naturally depend upon the extent of your garden, but it should be observed that any garden, however small, has a house in it, and that that house has walls. This is a very important fact to be remembered.

Often I hear people say, 'How lucky you are to have these old walls; you can grow anything against them', and then, when I point out that every house means at least four walls – north, south, east, and west – they say, 'I never thought of that.' Against the north and west sides you can grow magnolias or camellias; on the east side, which catches the morning sun, you can grow practically any of the hardy shrubs or climbers, from the beautiful ornamental quinces, commonly, though incorrectly, called Japonicas (the right name is Cydonia, or even more correctly, Chaemomeles), to the more robust varieties of *Ceanothus*, powdery-blue, or a blue fringing on purple. On the south side the choice is even larger – a vine, for instance, will soon cover a wide, high space, and in a reasonable summer will ripen its bunches of small, sweet grapes (I recommend Royal Muscadine, if you can get it); or, if you want a purely decorative effect, the fast-growing *Solanum crispum*, which is a potato though you might not think it, will reach to the eaves of the house and will flower in deep mauve for at least two months in early summer.

And apart from these wall-plants, many small trees may be set in convenient places. The flowering cherries and crabs have fortunately become a feature of most gardens, and how gaily they contribute to the aspect of English villages and cottages during the spring. Many of them, however, tend towards a rather crude pink; and those who would wish to avoid this colour may be better advised to plant the subtler greenish-white cherry called Ukon (*Cerasus Lannesiana grandiflora*) or the white-blossomed crab *Dartmouth*, with purplish-red fruits of remarkable beauty in the autumn; or that other crab, *Niedzwetzkyana*, with even more beautiful purple fruits. The almond, of course, will always be a favourite, partly because it flowers so early in the year; but if you are thinking of planting almonds now I would strongly recommend the variety called *Pollardii*, with a finer and deeper flower than the common kind usually seen.

The advantage of trees and shrubs is that they may be underplanted with bulbs – another activity which should not be neglected at this time of year. Daffodils, narcissi, and hyacinths should be got into the ground without delay. Bulbs are always a good investment, as they increase underground and may be lifted yearly, and the little offsets or bulbils planted out in a spare corner to develop. Such raising of one's own stock is much more satisfying than writing a cheque or buying a postal order.

September 3, 1950

Reproachful letters reach me: how *can* I say that the August garden is dull and heavy? These letters are all courteous and kindly, but it is evident that their writers are pained. Several of them paint a picture of such gaiety that I remain abashed. It is, of course, perfectly true that if you have time for the annuals (and not too large a space to fill) you can have a blaze of colour lasting well into September. It was not difficult to visualize the swagger patches that my correspondents were looking at: petunias, ageratum, snap-dragons, portulaca, cosmea, arctotis, larkspur, stocks, verbena, zinnias . . . the very

thought of them made me blink. And to these must be
added such perennials as the heleniums, the flat-headed
yellow achillea, the rudbeckias, the gaillardias (there are
two particularly fine ones, called *Tangerine* and *Wirral
Flame*). And dahlias. And gladioli. And montbretia. Yes,
perhaps I was wrong. I was probably thinking more of
the sluggish trees, the overgrown hedges, the brambles
bringing their first hint of autumn; and thus must
acknowledge that my aversion to the August garden
may be psychological rather than factual. I just cannot
bear feeling that summer is petering out to its end, and
spring so far behind.

As I have indicated, I don't grow many annuals except
the zinnias, to which I am always faithful. There is,
however, one which proved very decorative this year
and remained in flower for a very long time; in fact, it is
flowering still. This was *Venidium fastuosum*, a half-hardy
South African daisy of enormous size, three inches wide
at least, of the most brilliant, varnished-looking orange
petals and a central ring of darkness round the base.
Why, I wondered, looking into the heart of this garish
thing, should Nature take so much trouble and display
such inventiveness? Why such superfluous ingenuity?
Why this eternal, inexplicable miracle of variation? Was
it intended to appeal to us as human beings or to some
insect in search of nectar?

There are hybrids of *Venidium* which should be worth
trying, though *V. fastuosum* is probably the best. The
hybrids are described in catalogues as ranging in colour
from white to lemon and straw; there is also a dwarf
strain, about a foot high, in yellow and orange. If one

has facilities for starting them early, in boxes under glass, as is the usual practice with half-hardy annuals, they would, of course, come earlier into flower; but otherwise a sowing made out of doors towards the end of May, where they are intended to remain, would start flowering at the beginning of July and should continue right through August.

October

October 12, 1947

A new pleasure has abruptly entered my life, and I should like to pass it on to others: the Strawberry grape. It is perfectly hardy here in Kent, where an outdoor specimen, twenty years old, covers a cottage, and is now heavy with ruby-pink bunches this autumn even after the cruel winter of 1946–47. My own little vine is only in its second year, but is already fruiting so generously that a number of bunches had to be suppressed; it would have been unwise as well as unkind to let so young a thing carry more than eight. But I foresee that it will go on in strength and wealth.

The great point about this grape is its flavour. I hope the professional nurseryman will forgive me if I say that his claims for his wares sometimes read better on paper than they turn out in fact; his colours blow brighter, his fruit tastes sweeter, and the vigour of his plants is beyond belief. But the Strawberry grape really does taste of strawberries – the little Alpine or wood strawberry. One unkind guest said it tasted of peardrops, but I stick to my conviction.

A single plant will cost you 10s. 6d., but will, I am sure, prove an investment paying a good dividend. It can be obtained from The Six Hills Nursery, Stevenage, Hertfordshire.

Another vine which is giving me great pleasure at the moment is *Vitis heterophylla*, an East Asian. You can't eat it, but you can pick it and put it in a little glass on your table, where its curiously coloured berries and deeply cut leaves look oddly artificial, more like a spray designed by a jeweller out of dying turquoises than like a living thing. Yet it will grow as a living thing, very rapidly, on the walls of your house, or over a porch, hanging in lovely swags of its little blue berries, rather subtle, and probably not the thing that your next-door-neighbour will bother to grow or perhaps doesn't know about. There are some obvious plants which we all grow: useful things, and crude. We all know about them. But the real gardener arrives at the point when he wants something rather out of the common run; and that is why I make these suggestions which might turn your garden into something a little different and a little more interesting than the garden of the man next door.

A note on some special small trees for autumn colour may therefore not come amiss. *Cratægus Crus-Galli*, the Cockspur Thorn, turns as scarlet as you could wish in October, and is a tough little tree which will flourish anywhere; against the dark background of a hedge he will look splendid. *Disanthus cercidifolius* hangs itself with round leaves like golden coins. *Cornus Kousa* and *Cornus florida rubra*; *Berberis Thunbergii atropurpurea splendens*; *Parrotia persica*; *Prunus Sargentii*; all these will flame throughout October until the leaves come off. It is a good plan to plant them where at some moment of the day they will catch the sunlight; and it is more effective to plant two or three in a clump than some isolated specimen. This advice applies to most plants, but especially to those designed to make a bonfire of colour in the rich, mellow days of autumn.

October 30, 1949

It always surprises me that we in this country should neglect to plant some of the fruits which are now seldom to be seen save as survivals in some old garden. For example, the common quince. In some parts of France you see it growing as a hedgerow plant, its great yellow pear-shaped fruits heavily hanging for any thrifty villager to pick and turn into jelly or quince-cheese. It grows in the hedgerows there as thick as blackberries in an English lane. Why don't we plant it in our gardens here, as our grandfathers did?

It is of the easiest possible cultivation, and will do in almost any type of soil, though naturally it will be happiest in a nice light loam with plenty of humus. It appreciates moisture, so long as it is not completely waterlogged. It requires no pruning or spraying. So far as I know, it suffers from no form of disease. It is self-fertile. Birds do not attack it, and the fruit ripens too late for the wasps. The blossom comes late, and thus seldom has to endure danger from frost. It lives to a great age and is a regular and reliable cropper. It makes all the difference to stewed apples or to an apple-pie. It can, and should, be turned as I have said into delicious jelly, marmalade, or cheese. If it is on its own roots, as it usually is, it can be readily increased from its own suckers. To this catalogue of excellences, add that it is very beautiful, both in May when it flowers and in October when it ripens, and you will not wonder that I should demand a revival of planting the common quince.

So far as its beauty goes, I think there are two ideal situations to choose for it. One would be near water, so that the branches would hang over and be reflected in a pool, a stream, or even a pond. The other would be immediately beneath a bedroom window, so that in the spring you could look down into the wide upturned faces of the shell-pink blossom amongst the young leaves and the wiry tangle of very black twigs, and in the autumn on to the fat golden fruits. Only the occupant of that upper room could tell the delight of observing the quince throughout the cycle of the seasons.

Then, as a postscript, I might put in a good word for the bullace. This, like the quince, is a tree seldom seen except in old gardens. It is, I believe, the child of a marriage between a damson and a plum. It has no ornamental value, but crops inordinately every year, small purple fruits which bring a good marketing price if you have the patience and leisure to pick them, and can also be used to make bullace wine.

As for the cherry-plum, or *myrobalan*, the medlar, and the various gages, including the old greengage, I must leave those for another article.

October 1, 1950

I know I am continuously grousing about the dearth of plants, apart from annuals and herbaceous stuff, to enliven the garden in August and September, so it was with a startled pleasure that I observed three bushes growing in a cottage garden as I drove along a secret lane. They looked like pink lilac. Tall, pyramidal in shape, smothered in pointed panicles of flower, they suggested a bush of pink lilac in May. Yet this was September . . . Puzzled, I stopped by the roadside to investigate.

It was *Hydrangea paniculata grandiflora*, sometimes called the plumed hydrangea. In its native country, Japan, it is said to attain a height of twenty-five feet, but in this country it apparently limits itself to something between six and eight feet; and quite enough, too, for the average garden. Do not confuse it with *H. hortensis*, the one which sometimes comes sky-blue but more often a dirty pink, and which is the one usually seen banked up in Edwardian opulence against the grandstand of our more fashionable race-courses. *H. paniculata grandiflora*, in spite of its resounding name, is less offensively sumptuous and has a far subtler personality.

It reveals, for instance, a sense of humour, and even of fantasy in the colouring it adopts throughout its various stages. It starts off by flowering white; then turns into the pink I have already described as looking like pink lilac. Then it turns greenish, a sort of sea-green, so you never know where you are with it, as you never know where you are with some human personalities, but that makes them all the more interesting. Candidly white one moment; prettily pink the next; and virulently green in the last resort . . . As I was leaning over the gate, looking at this last pink-green inflorescence, the tenant of the cottage observed me and came up. Yes, he said, it has been in flower for the last three months. It changes its colour as the months go by, he said. He knew it was a hydrangea, though he couldn't remember its second name. He was very proud of it. He was a dark man, a foreigner: and although he spoke fluent English he had a thick, peculiar accent which I could not identify. As I was talking to him across his gate, a circus passed with all its caravans and roundabouts; and I thought that the foreign man, and the circus, and the English cottage garden were all very much of the same thing; and that I would certainly order *H. paniculata grandiflora* to grow in a damp, shady spot next year, and hoped it would do as well as his.

October 22, 1950

In my garden I have an awkward little border. It is awkward only in the sense that I have never made up my mind how best to use it. I have tried many things, and nothing has ever looked right, except the wine-coloured and ruby-coloured wallflowers in the spring. These have to be torn out towards the middle of May, when they are over and the little border is then left blank and empty, piteously clamouring for something to restore life to it during the summer. My little border, about a yard wide, happens to run along the foot of an old wall, this garden being largely a walled garden; but there are many narrow borders running under the house-wall, warm and sheltered, where one would wish to make the gayest possible display from April up to the autumn. The wallflowers are *right*; but what comes later? I have tried Korean chrysanthemums; no, they were too tall. I have tried annual carnations; no, they were too floppy. So now I have had another idea.

It was suggested to me by coming again across that pretty word: mixty-maxty. The dictionary defines it as 'incongruously or promiscuously mingled; jumbled together mixed; confused'. Very well, I thought, a mixty-maxty border it shall be. I will buy many packets of annuals, and sow them on the ground as soon as the wallflowers have been thrown away; but I shall not sow them according to the usual method, a patch of larkspur at the back, a patch of candytuft at the front, all regulated by their different heights and colours; I shall tear open all my packets and pour all the seeds out into an old tobacco tin, and shake them up together, and then sow them and let them take their chance. Very odd effects may result. I may get a tall spire coming up in front, and a dwarf hidden at the back, but I shall not care. The fun of gardening is nothing unless you take reckless risks.

All the same, despite recklessness, one must also be sensible. Let us now come down to brass tacks. One must draw up a list of annuals for sowing. One might include some half-hardy annuals, since they will not be sown until the latter half of May. Here is a rough draft of my list, my half-sensible, half-temerarious list, of the seeds I propose to order and shake up in a tin and scatter broadcast along that narrow border. They are all seeds which can be obtained at a very low price from any of the big seedsmen.

Phacelia campanularia. Cornflower. Salpiglossis. Zinnias. Cosmea. Coreopsis. Clarkia. Eschscholtzia. Love-in-a-mist. Petunias. Godetia. Salvia patens. Scabious. Larkspur. Verbenas.*

October 29, 1950

October is the time for the garden to be taken to pieces and replanted if necessary for next year. It is also the month that ushers in the long dark evenings when one makes seed lists under the lamp, pure pleasure and no worry; no slugs, no rabbits, no moles, no frosts, no damping-off. An interesting and unusual plant which should find a place is *Cobaea scandens*, which sounds more attractive under its English name of cups-and-saucers. This is a climber, and an exceedingly rapid one, for it will scramble eight to ten feet high in the course of a single summer. Unfortunately it must be regarded as an annual in most parts of this country, and a half-hardy annual at that, for although it might be possible with some protection to coax it through a mild winter, it is far better to renew it every year from seed sown under glass in February or March. Pricked off into small pots in the same way as you would do for tomatoes, it can

* July 1951. Do not follow this advice. It was a complete failure.

then be gradually hardened off and planted out towards the end of May. In the very mild counties it would probably survive as a perennial.

It likes a rich, light soil, plenty of water while it is growing, and a sunny aspect. The ideal place for it is a trellis nailed against a wall, or a position at the foot of a hedge, when people will be much puzzled as to what kind of a hedge this can be, bearing such curious short-stemmed flowers, like a Canterbury Bell with tendrils. Unlike the Canterbury Bell, however, the flowers amuse themselves by changing their colour. They start coming out as a creamy white; then they turn apple-green, then they develop a slight mauve blush, and end up a deep purple. A bowl of the mixture, in its three stages, is a pretty sight, and may be picked right up to the end of October.

If you are now thinking that a half-hardy annual such as *Cobaea scandens* is too much trouble, and perhaps want something more permanent than you can get out of a seed packet, do consider the rose called *Nevada*. It got an Award of Merit from the RHS in 1949, and well it deserved it. I do not think I have mentioned it before, and as it is a fairly new rose, you may not have come across it. This is not a climber, but a shrubby type, forming an arching bush up to seven or eight feet in height, smothered with great single white flowers with a centre of golden stamens. One of its parents was the Chinese species rose *Moyesii*, which created a sensation when it first appeared and has now become well known. For those who are interested in such pedigrees, the other parent was *La Giralda*, a cross between that grand old

Hybrid Perpetual, *Frau Karl Druschki*, and *Mme Edouard Herriot*. The grievance against *Moyessii* is that it flowers only once, in June; but *Nevada*, unlike *Moyesii*, has the advantage of flowering at least twice during the summer, in June and again in August, with an extra trickle of odd flowers right into the autumn. One becomes confused among the multitude of roses, I know, but *Nevada* is really so magnificent that you cannot afford to overlook her. A snowstorm in summer, as her name implies. And so little bother. No pruning; no staking; no tying. And nearly as thornless as dear old *Zéphyrine Drouhin*. No scent, I am afraid; she is for the eye, not for the nose.

November

November 24, 1946

Judging by the number of letters I received, my recommendation to plant the Alpine strawberries seems to have aroused some interest among readers of *The Observer*: I now venture, therefore, to recommend the hardy vine, or outdoor grape. I did just refer to this in an earlier article, but as a wall-covering rather than as a fruit, laying very little emphasis upon its edible qualities. It does not appear to be generally known that vineyards were once common in the southern counties, that the grapes ripened, and that wine was made from them; so that what man has done once, man can do again.

The wine-making part is of dubious value to-day, when wine-making means sugar; but there is no doubt that vines producing small, sweet bunches may profitably be grown against a south wall, say the wall of the house. There are several varieties which may be relied upon to ripen in any normal English summer – the non-summer of 1946 was, in fact, the only summer in which my grapes went mouldy, or shrivelled, or in some other way made themselves entirely useless. Of the several varieties I would recommend, in order of merit, *Royal Muscadine*, *Muscatel*, *Golden Drop*, *Dutch Sweetwater*. *Royal Muscadine* I have found by far the best, though *Muscatel* runs it close.

Royal Muscadine, moreover, has a romantic history: it was discovered at Cahors by Henry of Navarre on his way to Paris to become Henry IV of France, and was taken by him from Cahors to Fontainebleau, where it became known as the *Chasselas de Fontainebleau*. It is a Chasselas grape, meaning an ordinary little greenish grape of the type you see so plentifully displayed in greengrocers' shops in France and Italy, but none the worse for that, if you have the patience to pick it off berry by berry, or are so impatient as to cram a whole handful of berries into your mouth at one go. It is well worth growing in our southern counties against a warm wall for it means that you can pile a dish of grapes in August and September on your breakfast table.

The hardy vines are also very useful for making vinegar. You can use any of the hardy fruiting vines for this purpose, but if you want to obtain the real red wine vinegar I would recommend planting *Vitis vinifera Brandt*. This produces a dark, almost black grape, which turns into vinegar by the simple method of squashing the fruit into a wooden tub, leaving it to ferment for ten days or a fortnight, and then straining off the juice into bottles. Do not cork the bottles; put in a twist of paper to keep out the dust and flies.

Figs and peaches will likewise ripen in the south more readily than is sometimes supposed. There is no need to regard them as luxury fruits. The figs *Brown Turkey* and *Brunswick* are especially reliable against a wall.

A small shrub which I should like particularly to recommend is *Caryopteris Clandonensis*. It flowers from

August onwards, bright blue and fringed, at a time when flowering shrubs are rare. Prune it, not very hard, at the end of February, and it will make a rounded bush from three to four feet high. If you cannot obtain the variety *Clandonensis*, the sorts named *Mastacanthus* or *tangutica* will do as well. They like a sunny place but are not fussy as to soil; and in order to obtain the best effect I should plant at least three in a clump. At present-day prices, they cost from 4s. 6d. to 5s. 6d.

By the way, are you aware that many of the nursery-men now supply plant-tokens in the same way as book-sellers supply book-tokens? The only difference is that whereas book-tokens can be exchanged in almost any book-shop, plant-tokens can be exchanged only at the nursery that issues them; but as the big nurseries have a wide choice of plants and seeds, this restriction does not much matter.

November 13, 1949

I have been getting myself into trouble, and must put it right. Writing about quinces, I said that they were not liable to disease, *so far as I knew*. By that cautious little phrase I hoped to safeguard myself, and indeed my own experience of quince trees and all the books I consulted endorsed my opinion. It now appears that I was wrong. It appears that they are occasionally liable in wet sum-mers to 'a fungus rejoicing in the name of *Entomosporium maculatum*', which attacks both the foliage and the fruit; also to brown rot, which attacks the fruit; also to a fungus called cluster cups, which attacks the leaves and fruit of both the quince and the medlar. This fungus has an alternative host in the Savin juniper, and spores from the juniper can infect the quince and medlar, or vice versa. The moral obviously, and for once an easy one to observe, is to refrain from planting a Savin juniper in the near neighbourhood. I am much indebted to the East Malling Research Station for all this information.

The medlar is not a fruit I care much about; by the time it is ready to eat, it bears far too close a resemblance to a rotting or 'bletted' pear. It can, however, be made into a preserve, and the little tree certainly has a definite garden value, for in a favourable autumn the leaves turn into a motley of very beautiful variegated colours – pink, yellow, green, and brown, freckled with the russet fruits which always remind me of those knobbly objects you see attached to leather thongs on the flail-like hand-weapons of medieval warfare.

But although I may have no great affection for the medlar as a fruit, my affection for the cherry-plum or *Myrobolan* knows no bounds. I wish it could be planted more widely. It has every virtue. It grows quickly; it is pretty in the spring, with its white blossom; it reaches its supreme beauty when its fruit ripens in mid-summer and its branches droop with the weight of fruit almost to the ground. The branches then seem loaded with fat jewels of amber and topaz, like a tree in an oriental fairy-tale.

It crops generously, most years. Its fruit makes delicious jam, especially if you put in the kernels of the stones, when you get a sharp almond flavour, reminding you of kernels left in apricot jam. It also makes a good hedge. It is, I feel sure, a tree to plant both for your immediate pleasure and for the pleasure of your children after you.

Plant the gages, too. The old greengage and all the other gages, the *Cambridge*, the *Early Rivers*, the *Transparent*. This (November) is the time to order and plant them.

November 19, 1950

What, I wonder, do you feel about rock-gardens? Personally, I am against them, even when they are on a very grand scale. They seldom look right. Of course, if your garden happens to include a disused quarry there is nothing you can do but make a rock-garden out of it; but few of us are thus favoured. Most of us are reduced to some lumpy bank, over which we dispose all the oddments of old stone we can collect and plant them up with such common tufts as aubretia and yellow alyssum. It will be an artificial thing, pretending to be something it isn't.

Nevertheless, there is something to be said for rock-gardening provided you do it tactfully and do not pretend to be reproducing a bit of the Alps or the Himalayas or one of the more remote valleys of China where they were never intended to occur. The best claim to be made for rock-gardening is that it enables you to grow things according to the conditions which please them best. You can, in short, make up pockets of soil between the stones to suit individual plants. You can make a pocket of pure leaf-mould for *Gentiana sino-ornata*. You can make a sharp, gritty, sunny pocket for South African bulbs, the *ixias*, for example, or for the Mexican *tigridias*. You can fill one pocket entirely with limy rubble to please your dianthus; and another pocket with peat and leaf-mould to please your shrubby daphnes. In this way you can cut plants off, one from the others. You can prevent them from getting lost, as small things are apt to get lost in the open ground, and can also control any invasive neighbour – a vegetable neighbour, I mean, not a human one or a feline one.

You will observe that not all the plants I have mentioned are Alpines. This is because I never can see why one should be mesmerized into believing that Alpines should be the only occupants of a rock-garden. The only rule to follow, I think, is that whatever looks right *is* right. Obviously, herbaceous plants will look wrong, and so will many of the annuals; but the pockets are ideal places for the small bulbs, nor is there any reason why they should not come up through a carpeting of saxifrage or androsace or arenaria or *Dryas octopetala* or the prostrate rosemary. I like to see the miniature narcissi grown in such a way, and the striped Lady Tulip (*T. Clusiana*), and our native yellow tulip, *Sylvestris*, and the little green-and-white *Tulipa tarda*, sometimes called *dasystemon*, and that lovely Greek, *Tulipa orphanidea*, and the scarlet Persian *Tulipa linifolia*; and some fritillaries, too, not only our native Snakes-head, *Fritillaria meleagris*, but also *F. pyrenaica*, with its odd colouring of bronze

and green; and, of course, the little early Iris *reticulata*.
But I must desist. The bright picture growing up so rapidly
in my mind already threatens to exceed the canvas
allowed me.

November 26, 1950

A week ago I was writing in this column about rock-
gardens. Wildfire ideas swept across me, like a prairie
alight. My own small blaze was not comparable to that.
I just got excited about the things one could do in a
rock-garden, which is a mild little thing to get excited
about; but, after all, the point is not what you get excited
about, but the fact that in middle age you can still get
excited at all. There is nothing like gardening to keep
one young. It is the most rejuvenating of all occupations.
One is always looking forward to next year, or five years
hence.

I thought I would write this time about dry-wall
gardening. Fortunate indeed are those whose lot is cast
in one of our counties where low stone walls solidly
crammed with soil already form part of the local landscape – in the Cotswolds, for instance. But even if you
do not live where you may hope to find a ready-made
dry wall, there is no reason why you should not build
one in a place which seems to demand it.

A dry wall, it seems scarcely necessary to say, is a wall
in which no hard mortar is used to fix the stones, but
only soil to set them.

A retaining wall is the ideal, holding up a bank or a

terrace, because then you will be able to build it with a *batter*, which in gardening terms does not mean a sort of Yorkshire pudding but a receding slope, lying backwards from bottom to top; this gives strength to the wall, which, if it were upright, would almost certainly fall down in course of time. Tilt each individual stone slightly backwards also, choosing the biggest stones to set along the foot. Fill the space at the back of the wall with good soil, a mixture of fibrous loam (well-rotted turves are excellent), some sharp sand, some peat, and compost if you have it, and also pack every crevice with the same mixture as you go. The more crevices you are able to leave, consistent with safety, the better.

It is a good plan to put in your plants while you build, and far easier and more satisfactory than poking them in afterwards. It enables you to spread out the roots instead of cramming them, and also to water them in, should the weather be dry. Some sort of planting plan in advance is advisable, to get the colours right, and also the shape and habit of the various plants; for example, if you decide to grow some of the *Lewisias*, or the long-sprayed saxifrage known as *Tumbling Waters*, you will not want them to get smothered eventually under a great beard of aubretia.

December

December 22, 1946

I find, and do not doubt that most people will agree with me, that November and December are quite the bleakest months of the year for finding 'something to pick for indoors'. A flowerless room is a soul-less room, to my thinking; but even one solitary little vase of a living flower may redeem it. So in this note I propose to suggest some things that everybody can grow with a prophetic eye on next winter so that the usual blank period may not occur again. These will be things that flourish out of doors. I am not here concerned with greenhouses.

Viburnum fragrans will start producing its apple-blossom flowers in November, and unless interrupted by a particularly severe frost will carry on until March. It is a shrub growing eventually to a height of ten or twelve feet; it is extremely hardy; easy-going as to soil; and has the merit of producing a whole nursery of children in the shape of young self-rooted shoots. Picked and brought into a warm room, it is very sweet scented.

The Christmas roses, *Helleborus niger*, are in flower now. They don't like being moved – in gardening language, they 'resent disturbance' – so even if you will take my advice and plant some clumps in early spring, which is the best time to move them, directly after they have finished flowering, you may have to wait a year or two before they begin to reward you with their greenish-white flowers and their golden centres. They are worth waiting for, believe me.

They like a rather shady place; moist, but well drained. A western aspect suits them. Once planted, leave them alone. They will grow in strength from year to year. I have a plant in my garden which to my certain knowledge has been there for fifty years. It was bequeathed to me by an old countrywoman of the old type, who wanted me to have the enjoyment of it after she had gone.

Hamamelis mollis. This is the Witch-hazel, a small tree which begins to flower on its bare branches in January. It is a real tough, which will grow anywhere – any soil, any aspect – though the better you treat it the better it will do. This applies to most plants, as to most people. The Witch-hazel will give you scented twigs for picking at a very early age.

Then there is *Prunus autumnalis subhirtella*. This is a little tree which, as its name suggests, ought to flower in autumn. As a matter of fact, in this country it flowers in November or December, and is very useful on that account. Pick it in the bud; bring it indoors; and it will open into a fountain of bridal-looking blossom. It is said to strike very easily from cuttings taken in early summer from the current year's growth. I prefer it grown as a bush, not as a standard.

I should like to put in one last word for that very common plant, the pink-flowering currant, *Ribes sanguineum*. Nothing could be easier to grow, and it is sometimes despised on that account; but those who have the wit to cut some long stems of it in January, and to keep them in water in a dark cupboard, and to bring them out into the light in March, will find not a pink but a snow-white sheaf, a bride's sheaf, to reward them.

December 3, 1950

Many people have a limited garden space. They want to make the best of it and to get as much colour and variety as possible, yet the area they command restricts them. They have perhaps a front garden with a path running up it to the front door, and on either side of this path they have either a lawn of grass or some flower-beds, or both; and under the house they may have other beds, with a path running horizontally from left to right. This does not leave much scope for extra plants. I suggest, therefore, that gardening in tubs might be helpful, interesting, and amusing.

You acquire your tubs – barrels sawn in half. I would not paint them in the conventional colour, which in this country seems to be a most virulent arsenic green, swearing violently with all the greens of Nature; I would paint them the colour of coffee with far, far too much milk in it; and I would paint the bands round them the colour of coffee with no milk at all. This neutral coloration makes a much better foil to the colour of flowers than that wicked green.

You must now fill your tubs. Good drainage is essential, meaning a number of holes bored in the bottom, and then a two-inch layer of broken crocks (old flower-pots smashed up), and then a thick layer of fibrous leaf-mould half the tub deep; and then on top of all that the main soil in which your plants will have to grow for years and years. Give them a rich diet. Turfy fibrous loam and some compost and some bone-meal or some hop-manure, and some sharp sand to keep it open, all mixed up together. Fill the tubs to within two or three inches of the top, remembering that the soil will sink as it settles. Then the only thing left to do is to plant; and, of course, to water when watering becomes necessary. This is perhaps the only disadvantage of tub-gardening: you must keep a careful watch to see that your plants do not dry out.

Everyone will have his own ideas about what to grow. Some people will like tulips or other bulbs for the spring, followed in summer by annuals such as the purple petunia, which, sown in May, gives a sumptuous display from July to October. Others will prefer more permanent things such as fuchsias. Whatever you choose, tub-gardening does seem to be a solution for those who have not as much ground space as they would like and who, by setting their tubs where they want them, can prolong the flowering season in many odd corners.

December 17, 1950

Shady places often worry the amateur gardener, but, as a matter of fact, there are plenty of plants which thrive all the better for some shade. There are degrees of shadiness, and I suppose the ideal is a broken light, where the shadow is not too dense but is still sufficient to give protection from the hottest rays of the sun. In such a place, especially if the soil tends to be moist, all the coloured primroses and polyantha will be happy as a groundwork; and, if really moist, should be the perfect home for the taller primulas such as the Japonica hybrids, or the mealy mauve *P. capitata*, or the yellow Tibetan *P. Florindae*, or the coppery *P. Bulleyana*. These are all very easily raised from seed or division. Phlox enjoy shade and a deep, cool soil; so do the peonies. The columbines will put up with quite a lot of shade, and there are some very beautiful hybrids: *Longissima*, a fantastically long-spurred golden yellow; *Crimson and Gold*; *Crimson Star*; and a huge-flowered blue and white called *Azure Fairy*. Foxgloves are perhaps too obvious to be worth mentioning, but these also can be obtained now in different varieties: the Excelsior strain which flowers all round the stem, and the really lovely one called *Apricot*, well named, because it is exactly the pinky-amber of a ripe apricot turning its cheek to the sun. I think also that the pure white foxglove looks very handsome in a clump, towering above the colour of lower flowers. All obtainable from Messrs. Sutton.

If you prefer shrubs for your shady corner or border, the choice is wide. Azaleas, provided you have a lime-free soil; rhododendrons, which enjoy the same conditions, are mostly too space-taking for the average garden. Some of the daphnes are woodland, leaf-mould-loving plants, especially the murrey-coloured *D. mezereon* and its white form, *alba*; and *D. tangutica*; and the fine hybrid,

D. Somerset. And then there are the hydrangeas, many of which look far better, I think, shrouded in a little dusky mystery than exposed to a glaring light.

I have no room here to go into details about the hydrangeas; I wish I had. The best I can do is to recommend a book just published called *The Hydrangeas*, by Michael Haworth Booth (Constable, 26s.). He has spent many years in expert study, and this is the first specialized work to be written in the English language on the subject. Serious gardeners will feel compelled to add it to their gardening library; and those more frivolous gardeners, who like joky gardening, will delight in his paragraph on page 164, telling them how to produce miniature hydrangeas two inches high in pots.

December 24, 1950

This article will appear, I suppose, on Christmas Eve when nobody's mind is attuned to hard work out of doors. It therefore seems a suitable moment to take up the challenge of a gentleman in Staffordshire who wants me to write something in defence of Lazy Gardeners.

It is an amusing letter, quite indefensible, yet with some grains of truth in it. He toils not, he says, but all the same gets a lot of pleasure from his neglected garden. His trousers become golden with buttercup pollen as he walks across his unmown lawn. He stares out of his windows in astonishment that a fourpenny packet of seed could produce so many marigolds. He has had neither the time nor the energy to prune his rambler roses, but is enchanted to find that they are still flowering riotously. He enjoys the few perennials left by the previous tenant. In fact, he doesn't expect anything to grow and is thrilled when it does.

This not being at all my own idea of gardening, I gasped at first, but on reflection perceived that there was something to be said for his contentions. It was nearly true, as he remarked, that the lazy gardener has time, peace, and leisure to look at his garden, whereas the active gardener has only work and is far too busy to enjoy anything. It was true also, though he did not say this but only implied it, that tidiness could be overdone. Nobody likes to see nettles, docks, or ground-elder; but a certain disorder among the flowers is surely preferable to too rigid a regimentation. Staking, for example, is a thing which requires to be done with a rare tact; one does not want to see the tall asters beaten down in a sodden mass on the ground, but neither does one wish to see them bound to their stake like the head of a birch broom to its handle. As for grass, nothing can excel the beauty of perfect turf; but unless this can be achieved over a wide expanse, I like to see it enamelled with some daisies – not plantains, thank you, or dandelions.

My correspondent has formed the commendable habit of reading gardening books in the winter evenings, even if he has no intention of putting their instructions into practice, which reminds me that I am often asked to recommend a practical, straightforward, comprehensive book and have no hesitation in advising *The Amateur Gardener*, by A. G. L. Hellyer, published by Collingridge Ltd., price 25s. Even if this seems rather expensive I am sure it is worth the money. Eight hundred pages of text and many photographic illustrations.

December 31, 1950

This may seem an odd time of year to write about irises, those velvet-warm flowers we associate with June – the very word *June* warms me as I write it. Outside all is bleak; the grass looks starved and dingy; this wintry weather is as unbecoming to the garden as to the human face. We all looked pinched and shrammed. But the longest night and the shortest day have gone with December 21st; we have left our darkest days behind us.

These reflections have been induced in me by receiving a copy of the *Iris Year-Book*, published by the Iris Society. I suppose we all grow irises, of one sort or another, even if we are neither experts nor specialists. Most of the irises are the most obliging of plants, putting up with poor treatment, asking for little more than a place in the sun, a modest demand, which we should all enjoy if we could get it. All iris growers would be well advised to join the Iris Society, 10s. 6d. for the yearly subscription, which entitles the member to a free copy of the *Iris Year-Book*. Address: N. Leslie Cave, Summerlea, Sugden Road, Thames Ditton, Surrey.

I have written about irises in this column before now, but never, I think, have I mentioned the *Oncocyclus* and *Regelio* species. I hesitate to do so, because they are not so easy to grow, so I write this note only for gardeners who are prepared to take some extra trouble, quite a lot

of extra trouble. You should grow them on a raised bed
if possible, under a south wall, in very gritty soil with
lots of mortar rubble in it because they like lime and
good drainage; and mortar rubble supplies both. If you
have a warm, sheltered corner under a house wall, where
you can build up a little raised bed and fill it with the
sort of soil I have suggested, plant a few rhizomes of
Iris Susiana, the so-called Mourning or Widow Iris, a
black-and-white enormous flower, a fantastic flower that
doesn't look true, price about 2s. One calls it black-and-
white, but it is in fact grey veined with very dark purple,
as you can see if it is held up to the light. Seen like this,
the veining suggests an anatomical drawing; or, more
poetically, the leaden tracing in a stained-glass window.

Plant also a few rhizomes of Charon, or Hoogiana, or
Korolkowi. I do not pretend that you will get a lot
of bloom, and I do not deny that you may get some
disappointments, but the pride of your successes will
compensate. The main things to remember are: (*a*) good
drainage; (*b*) a sun-baking; (*c*) avoidance of damp in
summer, by placing a pane of glass over the dormant
rhizome. These irises come from desert countries, so
one must try to reproduce their natural conditions as
nearly as possible.